SEARCHING FOR GOD

A Journey into the Heart
of the Divine Mother

SEARCHING FOR GOD

A Journey into the Heart
of the Divine Mother

by DAYALU (TED ZEFF, Ph.D.)

SHIVA PUBLISHING
San Ramon, California

SEARCHING FOR GOD:
A Journey into the Heart
of the Divine Mother

PUBLISHED BY:
SHIVA PUBLISHING
P.O. Box 613
San Ramon, CA 94583

Cover Design by Alfred Rordame iv

ISBN 0-9660745-0-5

Permissions

Permission to reprint excerpts from the following is gratefully acknowledged:

Awaken Children, Volumes I-VII; Dialogues with Mata Amritanandamayi, by Swami Amritaswarupananda. Copyright 1995 by M.A. Center. Reprinted by permission.

Cosmic Chants, by Paramahansa Yogananda. Copyright 1938 by Self-Realization Fellowship. Reprinted by permission of Self-Realization Fellowship.

Come Quickly, My Darling Children!, by Marty Cottler. Copyright 1996 by Sierra Vista Publishing Co. Reprinted by permission

Holy Mother Amritanandamayi, pamphlet by M.A. Center. Reprinted by permission.

DEDICATION

How does one acknowledge and thank the Divine,
the Creator of all, who manifests in all sentient beings? Without God's grace and Ammachi's Divine love,
this book would never have been written.
Amma has given me hope when I have felt despondent, incom-
parable bliss when I've been in her presence,
and the discipline I so desperately needed
to help me focus on the goal of life,
which is to merge into God's infinite love.

ACKNOWLEDGEMENTS

This book could not have been written without the excellent editing skills of Shakti (Pete) Eriksson. I also appreciate the editing assistance of Indu (Veronica) Howell. I want to thank my parents, Dave and Sylvia Zeff, who taught me the importance of seeking spiritual truths. I also want to thank my son, David, who taught me innumerable life lessons. Finally, I want to thank all the devotees who allowed me to share their experiences with Ammachi.

TABLE OF CONTENTS

"Once upon a time, my soul was dancing in delight through the Path of Bliss.

At that time, all the inner foes such as attraction and aversion ran away, hiding themselves in the innermost recesses of my mind.

Forgetting myself, I merged in a golden dream which arose within me. As noble aspirations clearly manifested themselves in my mind, the *Divine Mother*, with bright, gentle hands, caressed my head. With bowed head, I told Mother that my life is dedicated to Her.

Smiling, She became a Divine Effulgence and merged in me. My mind blossomed, bathed in the many-hued Light of Divinity, and the events of millions of years gone by rose up within me. Then, seeing nothing as apart from my own Self, a single Unity, and merging in the Divine Mother, I renounced all sense of enjoyment.

Mother told me to ask people to fulfill their human birth. Therefore, I proclaim to the whole world the sublime Truth that She uttered, 'Oh Man, merge in your *Self*.'"

—Ammachi

PREFACE

If there is anything in this book which uplifts you spiritually it is coming from my beloved guru, Mata Amritanandamayi. However, if there is anything that you find disagreeable, it is due to my ego. I feel deeply blessed to have been able to receive direct guidance from a living master, Ammachi. There are so many spiritual teachers giving lectures in the West today that it may be difficult for some people to recognize when a fully enlightened master is really in their presence.

However, more and more people are recognizing Ammachi's greatness; that she is one with the Divine Mother of the Universe. Prior to her first world tour in 1987, she was totally unknown outside of India, yet today she now blesses hundreds of thousands of devotees throughout the world each year. This book is an account of my spiritual experiences from 1988 to 1997 with Amma.

ॐ

This book includes Sanskrit words and some unusual interpretations of English words. These words have been italicized the first time they appear in the book and are defined in the glossary. The quotes dispersed throughout this book that are in bold print are taken from *Awaken Children, Volumes I-VII; Dialogues with Mata Amritanandamayi.* The poems at the beginning of each chapter were composed by the author.

ॐ

The answers to the questions that Ammachi has given to the author were meant just for him and the reader should not assume that Amma would give the reader the same answers.

An Introduction
to Ammachi

Mata Amritanandamayi is an embodiment of unconditional love, devoted to the service of all humanity. People from all walks of life seek out the Mother, as she is affectionately called. She receives everyone in the same loving way, regardless of one's religious faith or non-belief. She welcomes all alike, from the wealthy executive to the leprous beggar, from the newborn infant to the wrinkled old man, from the hostile detractor to the ardent admirer. As an untiring servant of all people, her life is dedicated solely to removing the suffering of humanity. No one's concerns are insignificant to her.

Ammachi's motherly affection is a soothing balm to all who come to her. Taking each person to herself without reservation, she is like a mother with children, bringing solace and peace of mind to all. Her touch is so deeply moving that many burst into tears as they experience the radiance of her Divine love and compassion. She teaches by the example of her own life and conveys the highest spiritual truths in the simplest language. She has infused devotion to God, love for fellow beings and the spirit of selfless service into the hearts of millions.

Sudhamani (Ammachi's birth name) was born September 27, 1953 to an extremely poor but pious family in the lush state of Kerela on the Southwest coast of India. She is the fourth of eight surviving children. At her birth, her family was perplexed at the infant Sudhamani's dark blue complexion. Doctors ruled out disease and the blue hue on Sudhamani's skin gradually dissipated over the course of her first year. However, her family member's aversion to this incident marked the beginning of years of ridicule and abuse. Although as a child she underwent many severe hardships and encountered many obstacles, she sought solace in God.

Adding to the family's bewilderment was Sudhamani's early mastery of Malayalam, the region's local language. She began speaking at six months, and by age two, Sudhamani was singing songs and prayers in praise of *Krishna* without having received any formal instruction. At the age of five, she began composing songs of deep devotional significance. Her enchanting soulful singing became well known throughout the village. Amma has said,

> *"From childhood I had an intense love of the Divine Name. I would repeat the Lord's Name incessantly with every breath, and a constant flow of Divine thoughts was kept in my mind no matter the place where I was or the work I was doing."*

As the years passed, Sudhamani spent all of her free time immersed in meditation, longing for Krishna. People frequently found her sitting with eyes closed, softly singing to God with tears streaming down her cheeks. Although her family and many of the neighbors were religious, they did not understand Sudhamani's intense spiritual moods.

However, childhood friends readily gravitated to Sudhamani's playful, joyous, charismatic nature. After finishing her chores, she would tell friends spiritual stories about the playful child Krishna. At these times, her playmates would sing devotional songs composed by Sudhamani.

Required to work long hours in the service of her family, she could not continue attending school beyond the fourth grade. In addition to looking after all the family household chores, she served the elderly, poor, and sick in her seaside village as if they were members of her own family. She would often remove food and clothing from her family's home and distribute them to those who were poorer than herself. One day, not finding anything else, she gave away her mother's only gold bangle to a poor starving man. She received a severe beating when her father found out, yet she was happy that she could relieve someone's suffering.

Eventually Sudhamani was locked out of her house and had not even been given any food to eat. When sympathetic local women tried to bring her food and take care of her, they were sent away by the family. Some of the local villagers who could not understand her state of Divine bliss ridiculed her by throwing stones at her and placing thorns where she walked. Yet despite all these abuses, Sudhamani remained undisturbed, oblivious to the harassment and physical conditions. She slept outdoors; the sand was her bed, the stars her blanket and the moon her light. Animals came to feed her. In fact, a dog was seen bringing food packets to her in his mouth; and a cow stood near her so that she could drink from its udder.

One day in September 1975, Sudhamani overheard a family singing devotional songs to Krishna. She was immediately overtaken by Divine bliss as her appearance spontaneously transformed into the features and movements of Krishna. During the transformation, her skin hue became more blue like that of Krishna. This event marked her first manifestation of *Krishna Bhava,* the Divine mood of Krishna.

Many people assumed that Krishna had temporarily taken possession of Sudhamani in order to bless them, and news of this rapidly spread throughout the local villages. Skeptics abounded, and one of them demanded that Sudhamani perform a miracle as proof that she was indeed Krishna. She replied, "It is not my intention to show miracles. My goal is to inspire people with the desire for liberation through *realization* [the state of complete identity with God]. Miracles are illusory. That is not the essential principle behind spirituality. Not only that, once a miracle is shown you will desire and demand to see it again and again. I am not here to create desire but to remove it."

Yet out of compassion towards the villagers and to inspire them with faith, she asked one of the skeptics to bring a cistern of water. After a portion was distributed to the devotees, Sudhamani told the skeptic to dip his finger in what remained. To everyone's amazement, the water had turned to milk and the urn was full. The milk was then distributed among the crowd. Another skeptic was called up by Sudhamani, and he was instructed to dip his finger into the remaining milk. It was immediately transformed into a pudding made from milk, bananas, sugar and raisins. This too was distributed to the hundreds of people assembled. This event created a vast change in the minds of the people. From that day on large crowds gathered around her.

On another occasion, a devotee of Ammachi brought her an oil lamp for the little temple in which she received devotees, but her elder brother, one of her greatest antagonists, smashed it. Amma then asked the devotees to bring shells into which water was poured, and a wick was placed in each. She asked the people there to light them and the light from these shells lasted the entire night.

However, as the crowds grew larger to receive Sudhamani's blessings, the vehemence toward her behavior grew. An opposition movement felt threatened by her for not following the traditional role of a woman in India of marrying, bearing children and staying at home. They ridiculed her and plotted her death.

During Krishna Bhava the devotees would offer Sudhamani milk to drink. One day an atheist milk vendor secretly added poison to the milk that a devotee bought to offer to Sudamani. Although she knew the milk was poisoned, she did not want to upset the devotee so she drank it. For the remainder of the night, Sudhamani periodically became sick and interrupted Krishna Bhava darshan for a few minutes to vomit in private, but continued the program until every devotee received her blessing.

One day while Sudhamani was sitting alone in a meditative mood, a beautiful orb of brilliant light appeared before her. As she looked on in wonder, the Divine Mother emerged in an exquisitely beautiful form and then suddenly disappeared along with the light. This vision left Sudhamani with an intense desire to see the Divine Mother again. After many days of meditation and crying out, the Divine Mother at last reappeared and merged in her. Following this experience, Sudhamani withdrew herself from everything and everyone, and remained immersed in the intense inner bliss of God-Consciousness.

However, suddenly one day she heard a voice from within her say, "I am in all as the One Essence and do not have a particular abode. It is to give solace to the suffering humanity that you have come into this world and not merely for enjoying Divine Bliss. Therefore, worship Me by showing mankind the way back to Me." This was a turning point in Sudhamani's life. The following days found her identified with the loving Divine Mother and it was from this time onwards that people began calling Sudhamani "Mother" or "Ammachi."

Once she heard this call from the Divine Mother, approximately six months after the beginning of Krishna Bhava, Ammachi began manifesting Devi Bhava, the mood of the Divine Mother. Ammachi has said, "All the deities represent the infinite aspects of the One Supreme Being, which exist within us as well. A Divine personality can manifest any one of them by mere will for the good of the world. Devi Bhava is the manifestation of the Eternal Feminine, the Creatrix; the active principle of the Impersonal Absolute.

"It should be remembered that all objects having a name or form are mere mental projections. Why should a doctor wear a white coat or a policeman a uniform and cap? All these are merely external aids meant to create a certain impression. In a like manner, Ammachi dons the garb of Devi in order to give strength to the devotional attitude of the people. The Universal Spirit that is in me is also within you. If you can realize that Indivisible Principle that is ever shining in you, you will become one with That."

Mother in Devi Bhava.

Since 1981 the Holy Mother has been disseminating spiritual knowledge to a dedicated group of spiritual aspirants who have come to study with her, training them with practical spiritual discipline. She has stated that the greatest of all blessings is to rouse an aspirant to the glory of the Divinity within. Ammachi's work has blossomed into an international organization engaged in many spiritual and charitable activities.

Mother's compassion for the poor resulted in her assuming responsibility for a financially troubled orphanage near the ashram. More than four hundred children were starving and lived in filthy buildings on the verge of collapse. Ashram residents cleaned and improved the facility. Electricity and plumbing were installed and the children were fed nourishing food. With the material basics taken care of, a comprehensive educational program was instituted.

Mother also has been involved in starting a vocational training center, a computer training institute, and a hospice for the terminally ill. Mother's ashram is also providing housing, food and clothing to the poor. It was Amma's wish that a multi-specialty charitable hospital in Cochin, Southern India be created. The new 800 bed hospital, which will open in 1997 is dedicated to giving free comprehensive medical services to all in need regardless of race or religion.

CHAPTER I

My Early Experiences

I'm so sad my Lord,
show me the way home.
I'm caught in delusion, again and again.
Show me the way home,
into Thy infinite light.
Stop all my illusory games,
Show me the way home.

I can't stop my mind from coming up with one horrible thought after another," I obsessed as I fidgeted in bed trying to fall asleep. "I'm supposed to drive all the way to San Francisco tomorrow morning... wait make that in just five hours, to see that new spiritual teacher from India, and I'll never be able to drive so far without sleep... I might fall asleep at the wheel and get into an accident and die... I know, I'll drink coffee; but then I'll get all nervous and won't be able to sleep tomorrow night... I feel just as alone now, even after having been on a spiritual path for years, as I did when I was being teased in junior high.... All right, I need to relax... watch my breath go in and out.... Oh geez, I'm all wound up... O.K. watch the breath.... I'm still so anxious I just can't lie here.... Whom can I turn to?"

As I nervously tossed around in bed, I recalled a story about a man who had died asking St. Peter if God had really been with him during his life. The man looked down at the Earth and saw four footprints on the ground indicating that God was always walking beside him. However, during his most trying times, he saw only two footprints. He asked St. Peter why God abandoned him during his time of need. He was told that this was the time God had been carrying him. I thought that while I too felt so alone during most of my life, unknown to my "conscious" mind, Divine Mother had really always been with me. As I began contemplating that I really do have a Divine companion, I slowly drifted off to sleep.

Upon waking in the morning, I meditated on the Zen koan, "Am I really alone?" As I brushed my teeth, I looked up into the mirror and stared into my eyes. "Has God really been with me? God has been too amorphous a concept for me to grasp. I can relate to another human being made out of flesh and blood whom I can hold and talk to, but trying to communicate with and hold on to thin air—give me a break!"

Suddenly I was flooded with an early memory of when I was nine years old, standing totally still on my steep, ivy-covered front lawn in Atlanta. I knew that the house in front of me wasn't really my home. In my heart I felt that I was from a different place which was full of peace and harmony. I became completely detached from everyone and everything on the Earth plane. After some time, I slowly returned to body consciousness. When I tried to explain this experience to my mom, she simply dismissed it as having a dizzy spell.

I then recalled when I was six years old standing in the small 50's style kitchen of our modern home in the heart of Dixie as my mom prepared dinner and asking her how the Earth was created. Answering to the best of her ability, she would say God made the world. Then I would query where did God come from. She would simply respond that God has always been here.

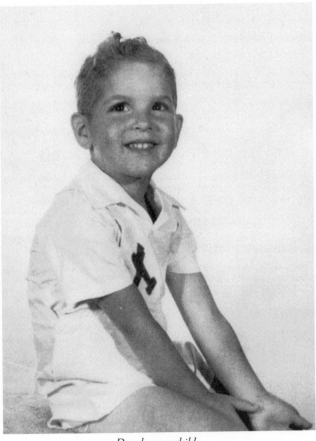

Dayalu as a child.

My little mind couldn't grasp the concept that God is omni-present. "How could there be no beginning or end?" I would ask in my deep Southern drawl. "Everything must have a beginning." Even as a first grader, I remember being awe-struck that there was something so big and omniscient that had always been here. I used to fall asleep at night thinking there was a gigantic, freck-led, compassionate boy hovering above the Earth who had the biggest puppet set in the Universe and he was pulling the strings of all the people on the Earth. I felt a sense of security drifting off to sleep, knowing that we were in good hands of this gentle boy with the giant puppet set.

Now, as I packed my suitcase, I pondered how I had always been searching to understand the meaning of life. As I carefully loaded my valise into the trunk of my Toyota sedan, I remem-bered as a child feeling a sense of inner peace and security sitting in the large, stain-glass, domed sanctuary of the synagogue lo-cated high up on a grassy knoll overlooking Peachtree Street. Al-though I didn't understand the meaning of the Jewish prayers and scriptures, I felt a sense of excitement thinking that there was some other being always protecting me as I fidgeted then on the soft, red, velvet cushion.

However, my sense of security in the ubiquitous protection of God exploded when I was twelve years old. One Sunday morn-ing as I ran toward the family two-tone green Pontiac with a golden Indian chief on the hood, I wondered which Bible story we would study that morning in Sunday school. I remember feeling a sense of awe and reverence reading about the powerful comic book-like, prophetic heroes in the multi-colored children's Bible. The ring of the telephone halted our weekly drive to the Temple by the news that our synagogue had been bombed by the Ku Klux Klan (like the scene depicted in the movie "Driving Miss Daisy"). My child-like faith in the protection of God had been shattered. I remember throwing a penny against the wall on which was written "In God We Trust" and deciding instead to believe that only human beings could make the world secure.

While driving to the Bay Area to visit this new spiritual teacher called Ammachi, I quickly became lost in the reverie of my childhood search for security and justice. I remembered whenever I raced to the brand-new, yellow school bus with the number #74 emblazoned on the front, all the children would shove to sit in the back of the bus because the ride was bumpier. The children would shriek with delight as J.B., our bus driver, purposefully drove over the ruts on Briar Cliff Road.

One time when I enthusiastically boarded the 16 Noble trolley car by myself to meet my dad downtown, I scampered to the back of the bus for another thrilling, bumpy ride. However, the ride turned out to be bumpier in unexpected and frightening ways.

As a color-blind child in the segregated South of the 1950's, I didn't understand why some people were squashed into the back of the bus. The eyes of the black people became filled with fear as they shouted for me to move on up to the front, scared that I was going to get them in trouble. A few bigoted white people shouted, "Get away from them Coloreds." Bewildered and afraid of the intensity of the emotion exhibited on the bus, I took my "correct" seat near the front door.

On another occasion, I witnessed a white bus driver close the door on an elderly black domestic worker, who after a hard day of ironing and scrubbing was getting on the bus too slowly. Once when my family was at the downtown bus station, I asked my dad why there was a separate water fountain that said "Colored." Being raised by liberal Northerners in a segregated South, I learned to feel deep compassion for the mistreatment of black people. However, when our family moved to New Jersey in my adolescence, I saw that the segregation and prejudice was identical, only disguised in a more subtle form.

The move to the North was painful and traumatic for me. I really missed the genteel Southern hospitality, polite behavior and relaxed lifestyle. I was shocked by the harsh and hostile environment that I encountered in the New York area. Was God's light really with me when I was a teenager? I surely had no idea of how to access the Divine during my lonely adolescence.

I thought of one bright spot for me: attending my Jewish youth group, the Jersey Federation of Temple Youth. Coming home from a youth conclave, I recall talking about God's love and repeating the holy Jewish prayer "Hear, Oh Israel: The Lord our God, the Lord is One." God's presence was expressed through doing good deeds (mitzvoth) for humanity. The Jewish tradition frequently focuses on compassion and helping the poor and less fortunate. I felt a sense of "joie de vivre" when I was able to serve the downtrodden and underprivileged.

As I exited the Bay Area freeway to fill up my gas tank on my way to see Ammachi, I noticed that the car in front of me was covered with Stanford University decals. I thought to myself, what about college? Did I feel less lonely and fearful there? I recalled how, so-cially, life improved for me as I entered Rutgers University but that spiritually I had become an agnostic. During my freshman year, I frequently argued spiritual concepts with a friend who attended Catholic schools all his life, as we sat in the basement fraternity house. I told him that there is no such thing as God; that people just make up the notion because they're afraid of facing the truth of how alone we really are; that when you die, that's the end of everything. My friend offered his best religious arguments for an afterlife but I could only respond, "If you're right and I'm wrong, I guess you'll be waving good-bye at my poor soul as you're risin' on up from the grave." However, I remember my agnostic beliefs being provoked by a quote that was carved into the desk in my intro to psychology class that read: "God is dead"—Nietzsche; "Nietzsche is dead"—God.

I felt so insecure from having experienced childhood abuse that I began trying to impress everyone with my material accom-plishments. I was able to acquire a new, black, sport Fury Ply-mouth convertible that had a red stripe down the side and red leather bucket seats; this was considered the epitome of "cool" in 1965. Cruising the campus with my fraternity brothers with the top down and the tachometer revved up, I tried desperately to get approval from my classmates. In a class discussion group, I recollect a student discussing how material comforts are only tem-porary while the real enjoyment in life is developing one's spiri-tual values. I contemptuously retorted "I feel pretty darn happy every time I get in my groovy convertible." A look of disgust slowly began to cover the student's face as the other materialists vali-dated how enjoyable it was to drive a cool car.

I then contemplated how my values during my college years only separated me further from God. After college, through fortuitous nepotism I was able to fulfill my military requirement (at the height of the Vietnam war) by serving for two years in Washington D.C. in the U.S. Public Health Corps. During the politicized late 60's and early 70's, my anger at having been hurt as a child was focused on those malicious right-wing Republicans trying to ship young people off to die in Vietnam.

Rather than taking responsibility for my actions, I tended to blame everyone but myself for my impertinent behavior. I remember thinking that I had nothing in common with the enraged man I saw at the department of motor vehicles screaming that he would be damned if the Governor was going to take any more money out of his pocket. Everyone standing in line was shocked to hear his angry verbiage. After the irate man exited the room, I sarcastically joked, "First it was my mother, then it was my father, and now it's the damn Governor that's causing all my problems."

While marching for outer peace against the Vietnam war, I neglected to walk internally for inner peace. Besides using the political system to release my early childhood anger, I also used politics to bolster up my weak ego. While I felt that it is very important for people to create peace in the world by working within the political process, I have since learned that it is important to first do the spiritual growing up and approach politics from a place of love.

In 1968 Senator Eugene McCarthy ran for president on an Anti-Vietnam War plank. He quickly became the hero of many college students who were supporting the U.S. withdrawal from Vietnam. My mother had been McCarthy's campaign manager when he first ran for congress in 1948 in Minnesota and his family had lived in our house in St. Paul. I quickly jumped on the McCarthy bandwagon as I rallied the campus to support "my friend," Gene.

Dayalu during the late '60s.

The following year I had attended a meeting in Washington D.C. chaired by the 1972 Democratic Presidential nominee, Senator McGovern, to reform the Democratic Party. I noticed Senator Muskie, who was the Vice Presidential Democratic candidate in 1968, enter the hearing and I had the chutzpah to show him a speech I wrote about the need to reform the Democratic party from a young person's perspective. Senator Muskie included my speech in his testimony that morning on Capitol Hill. Although my ego became quite pumped up thinking that I was so important interacting with famous politicians, the end result made me feel more alienated and lonely. My flash-in-the-pan fame only lasted for as long as I could tell the story to people and then I was forced to face the reality of my real emptiness.

During this time period, I read the book "Exodus" about the establishment of the state of Israel. At the end of my quasi-military stint, I decided to move to Israel. I thought that I would find happiness in this new country bursting with virtuous ideals and my Jewish tradition. I believed that this search for inner peace would be different from the others and I would find a purpose to my life. The reality of living in Israel in 1970 differed greatly from the life-style during the War for Independence in 1948. I brought my problems with me on the El Al plane to Israel. After six months, I became disillusioned and made my exodus back to New Jersey to study for a masters degree in counseling and began attending psychotherapy sessions.

After working for two years as a family social worker and completing a year of psychotherapy, I moved to the San Francisco Bay Area thinking that left-wing politics and working in an alternative school would give me fulfillment in life. While I enjoyed leaving middle class suburbia and was enchanted by the different ethnic and political groups in the Bay Area, my El Al airplane baggage was simply exchanged for a similar suitcase in a Datsun trunk which I drove across country.

Now, fifteen years later, as I drove to San Francisco again, munching away on some stale, preservative-laden cheese crackers, I thought to myself, "Here I go again, driving to the Bay Area to find peace and happiness." The continuous futile search for love and approval from human egos naturally wasn't satisfied by a three thousand mile change of residency.

I remembered how spiritual teachers have stated that everyone who says they will love you forever will eventually leave you; that only God will be with you forever. I thought of a song by Paramahansa Yogananda, the Indian saint who lived in the United States from 1920 until his passing in 1952, that states: "In this world, Mother, no one can love me. In this world they do not know how to love me. Where is there pure loving love? There my soul longs to be, there my soul longs to be."

When I moved to San Francisco in 1974, I began working in an alternative junior high school where the lesson plans for teaching children were innovative but the immature behavior of some of the teachers created much turbulence for adults as well as children. People in the school (like in most groups) were continuously fighting for control, feeling that their idea was right and the other person was wrong. I'm sure I was modeling horrendous behavior for the students by my need to always be right.

In 1976 I returned early from a trip to Paris to visit my parents who were residing in France. Although I had traveled to Europe on two previous occasions, I had a great deal of anxiety on this journey. My old childhood pain was restimulated by feeling trapped and powerless staying in my parent's small apartment in a foreign country. A panic reaction was triggered and I felt that I needed to return to California immediately.

However, I received a spiritual blessing when I arrived back in San Francisco ahead of schedule. I noticed a newspaper ad about a Ph.D. program in integral psychology at the California Institute of Asian (Integral) Studies where I could use my veterans benefits. I thought to myself, "Far out, I could take some interesting psych courses a few blocks from my apartment and even get paid for it." At the time I applied to the institute, I didn't realize that the school was based on the teachings of a great yogi from India, Sri Aurobindo. At that time in my life the only yogis I knew were Yogi Bear and Yogi Berra.

During my first night of class at the institute, we were supposed to share who our precursor was to arriving on an Eastern spiritual path and to discuss our impressions of the spiritual community in Auroville (in India). I wasn't sure what a "precursor" was and I thought Eastern spirituality meant back on the East Coast, so I proudly declared in my thick Jersey accent, "I read a book about bioenergetics in New Jersey." To impress my fellow students that I was familiar with California, I announced, " I took a trip last month up to Oroville where there's some great hiking trails" (as opposed to Auroville, India where a community based on Sri Auribindo's teaching was created).

I received some rather strange and bewildered looks from my classmates although the empathetic teacher, trying to make some spiritual sense out of my verbal blunders, told me, "It's all right to have a Western teacher." With deep insight, I responded, "Bioenergetics wasn't started on the West Coast but in New York." It wasn't until the end of the class that I realized how I had made an utter fool of myself. However, as I walked home that night skipping down Dolores Street in San Francisco, I experienced a deep sense of well-being that encompassed my entire being for the first time in my life. Unbeknown to me, it felt as if Sri Aurobindo's vibration touched my soul that evening.

Over the next seven years I jumped into learning about various spiritual approaches from Buddhist Vipassana meditation to Rajneesh's exotic techniques. To increase serenity in my life, I bought a physical isolation tank whereby I would float in saltwater in a tomb-like structure made with cardboard and a waterbed liner. In the dark, silent space where all stimuli was removed I would finally be able to enter a world of peace and tranquillity. However, when I would emerge from the tank, the inner peace soon evaporated in the noise of the honking, smog-producing buses and speeding police cars with their shrill sirens rising into my meditation room from the street below. I wrote my doctoral dissertation on the physiological and psychological effects of meditation and the physical isolation tank on Type A behavior. Unfortunately, my research only confirmed my personal experience that the long, sought-after peace derived from the tank was only temporary.

During this time I tried many new-age individual and group therapy techniques to create the joy that had been lacking in my life. My vedic astrology chart correctly indicates that with my turbulent emotional nature and the placement of Venus, I would have much chaos in relationships with women. However, I thought that if I could overcome my early childhood trauma and find the perfect woman to marry, I would be happy.

There is great pressure in this society on men: they are only considered a success if they marry a lovely lady and earn a lot of money. By subscribing to such mores, it has been rather difficult for me to listen to and follow my inner calling. The need to seek approval from all those people (living or dead or in various new forms) who humiliated me has created major obstacles to my progressing in my inner search for God.

My new spiritual and psychotherapeutic endeavors began to give me some tranquillity in my life. However, I still found myself repeating old negative behavior patterns with people. I frenetically searched for the perfect long-term relationship but was continuously frustrated by never achieving the "American dream." To avoid feeling like a loser, I desperately dove into superficial relationships in order not to be alone, especially on those most important of American holidays: New Year's Eve and Valentine's Day.

In October of 1983, I had been agitated and sad at the cumulative loss of several relationships and did not know where to turn for solace. As I was walking to meet a friend for lunch, a piece of paper blew in front of me as I walked by a health food store named "Back To Nature." I picked up the paper that was entitled "How To Be Happy." The article summarized Paramahansa Yogananda's teachings. Although I was familiar with Eastern philosophy, suddenly a magnetic force pushed the paper against my heart and I literally couldn't remove it for a few moments. The words seemed to jump out from the paper as I said to myself, "Yes, this is the way." The article further described a spiritual community based on Yogananda's teachings, located in the mountains of Northern California.

A mammoth traffic jam in front of the Golden Gate bridge jarred my awareness back to how late I would be for the program with that new woman spiritual teacher, Ammachi.... All right, just relax. I need to see the traffic jam as an opportunity to meditate on God... oh great, now I won't have time to even eat dinner before the stupid program begins... I knew I shouldn't have come....

As I anxiously crossed the bridge with the shimmering city lights staring at me, I took a deep breath and reminisced how I had moved from San Francisco to the spiritual community in the bucolic and majestic Sierra Nevada mountains where I then lived for eleven years. Residing amongst devotees in a placid, rural environment was just the antidote to my *rajasic* (hyperactive) worldly life-style. I finally began to do *sadhana* (spiritual practices) on a regular basis, as I meditated and chanted daily.

Over the years, my focus slowly began to shift from striving only for outer gratification to shifting to the realization that looking for God within was the most important desire in my life. There was nothing like living among like-minded spiritual seekers to help me dive deeply into my spiritual journey. I learned a modicum of self-discipline by following the teachings of Yogananda. I remember one incident of wanting to leave the community temple during a long meditation but forcing my restless mind and body to remain focused on God. Through perseverance, I stuck it out to the end of the meditation. The result: a rare, blissful inner experience.

As I gazed out at the beauty of God in nature near my mountain-top home, I would sing Yogananda's chant "Oh God Beautiful." Under a clear indigo sky, surrounded by immense oak and pine trees that overlooked a turquoise waterfall on the Yuba river, I would sing "Oh God beautiful, oh God beautiful at Thy feet I do bow, at Thy feet I do bow, oh God beautiful oh God beautiful, in the forest Thou art green; in the mountain Thou art high; in the river Thou art restless, in the ocean Thou art grave, oh God beautiful, oh God beautiful, at Thy feet I do bow, at Thy feet I do bow."

The view from my home in the Sierra foothills.

As I sat in the endless traffic jam on the bridge, I picked up a story from my car seat about a recent spiritual journey I had just written. The story described an experience two months earlier when I had let God, rather than my ego, guide me. I intended to read the story to my friend, Lynn, when I arrived in San Francisco. As I became bored sitting in the traffic, I began reading the story to myself out loud:

"Oh no, it must be after 2:00 a.m." I said to myself as I tossed in bed with beads of sweat dripping down my face. "I really shouldn't take such a long plane trip to Atlanta tomorrow morning. I ache all over and have a flu. What am I going to do?" Suddenly a saying by Paramahansa Yogananda came into my mind. "When boisterous storms of trial shriek and when worries howl at you, drown their noises by loudly chanting God, God, God."

I decided to sit up in my bed to pray and meditate. With all the fervor of my heart I prayed "Please help me Divine Mother. I'm not able to cope with such anguish alone. I can't sleep, I'm sick and don't know where to turn" After meditating for a few minutes, I unexpectedly became very sleepy. The pain and anxiety finally dissolved into the peace of Divine sleep.

As the light of the breaking dawn filled my cold bedroom, I opened my eyes and made a resolve that every step of my trip would be guided by God. I had lived in Atlanta and although my childhood memories were painful, there was a nebulous glimmer of excitement at the idea of spending a few days visiting the city where I had once lived. As I boarded the plane, I noticed my energy increasing and my aches and pains dissolve into the nothingness from where they came.

It had been a quarter of a century since I left the industrial capital of the South. When I arrived in Atlanta, I rented a car and drove to my old neighborhood. The suburb used to be located in the hinterlands but now it was renamed Midtown. Memories flooded my inner being: a reminiscent smell of grits cooking on a restaurant grill and the sweet scent of a pink dogwood tree in bloom. I had a recollection of my kind and gentle gray-haired second grade teacher, Miss Mabrey, whispering to me in her melodic Southern drawl.

As I drove up University Drive in my rental car, I exclaimed to myself, "That's my old house over there; the brick one with the large screen porch. Dad's ivy is still winding up the hillside." Down the road was where my friend, Irvin and I used to make the daily treks to Shackleford's drugstore in the summer to buy candy and baseball cards with pink, cardboard-like gum. We'd especially enjoy those little wax bottles filled with syrup and the Necco candy that we would fight over to see who would get the chocolate pieces. I wonder whatever happened to my good old friend Irvin who would always stand by me. I remember trying to find Irvin once when I visited Atlanta twenty years earlier back in the late 60's but his family had moved out of the neighborhood. I felt sad that I would never see my childhood friend again.

As I sat in the car, I turned inward and thought to myself, Divine Mother, what do you want me to do now? I felt guided to hike up to Shakelford's drugstore as Irvin and I used to do nearly three decades ago. I thought to myself, "There's the muddy creek where we used to play in that thick red Georgia clay. Dead Man's Hill still looks scary where I used to race my new, green, three-speed bike. There's my friend Bubba's house; I wonder how he's doing. Thank you Divine Mother for bringing me here." Returning to my car, I stared at the rose-covered mailbox where the name Mayer was written in wrought iron. Can it possibly be that the same neighbors still live next door?, I thought to myself.

I looked for that Southern charm and hospitality in the cold eyes of the white-haired woman who answered the door but I was greeted only with a curt, "Yes, can I help ya?"

"Pardon me, ma'am, my name is Ted Zeff and many years ago I used to live next door...."

Instantly, my old neighbor shouted with glee, "Teddy! Teddy! Hey Moe," she exclaimed turning toward her husband, "You're not going to believe who's here. It's little Teddy from next door all grown up! You just come right on in. How's your Mama and Daddy doin? You just gotta stay for dinner."

Entering the white, colonial-style home, I thought to myself, Divine Mother, what do you have in store for me now? "So anyway, Bubba was killed in a car crash about ten years ago and Mrs. Fine died when her house caught fire...."

"Excuse me, Mrs. Mayer, would you know whatever happened to Irvin?"

"Oh, he has a little shop over in Athens, Georgia about two hours from here," she replied, passing me a bowl of black-eye peas.

When I returned to my motel room, I thought how ridiculous it would be to call someone I hadn't talked to in nearly three decades. However, I really wanted to thank Irvin for having been my good friend. His having approved of me exactly as I was helped me keep a flame of self-worth burning within me all these years. Perhaps that bit of self-worth gave my soul the strength to seek God in this life. I remembered that before I left California, I asked Divine Mother to guide me on this trip. I'll put out the energy and if God wants me to find Irvin, so be it.

"I'm sorry but I have no listing in Athens for anyone by that name." O.K., I'll look in the local phone book and see if perhaps a relative knows his whereabouts.... Oh no, there are thirty listings with the same last name in Atlanta. I'm not going to call them all from a pay phone. All right, God, I'll call just the first name and if nothing materializes, I'll let go of the search.

"Irvin, that's my son," the surprised woman on the phone responded. As I hung up the phone, I knew I must keep following this Divine flow by calling the number that she gave me.

"Yes, this is Irvin."

"This may sound quite unusual but my name is Ted Zeff. I'm visiting Atlanta for the first time in twenty-five years and I used to have a friend with your name."

"What did you say your name was?" He responded in a bewildered Southern drawl.

"Ted Zeff," I replied softly.... Silence.... Oh, no... how embarrassing, the guy doesn't remember me.... Dead silence....

After a few moments of embarrassment, Irvin cautiously and vaguely volunteered, "I knew a Teddy from cross the street."

"Teddy, well that's me," I replied ebulliently.

"Golly! Golly! Teddy? Teddy?" Irvin excitedly shouted in his deep Southern drawl. "You just gotta come on out and visit me."

As I drove up the dirt road to my old friend's house, I was instantaneously struck by the similarity between his house and my California home.

"Hey, Teddy, " Irvin shouted as he came running down the porch stairs to greet me. I was trying to find some resemblance between the boyhood picture of us that I had brought on the trip and this personable middle-aged man.

All of a sudden a multitude of memories rushed through my consciousness. "Hey, Irvin, remember the funky clubhouse we all built? ...our secret meetings... and then we used to crawl up that big log on the 'desert'.... Remember how your brother put us down for being skinny and we snuck into your dad's workshop to pilfer his big old ax and chopped wood furiously to get big muscles?"

"Yeah Teddy, I remember all that. Hey, what about those jungle games we used to play down by the creek? Boy, we really had a lot of fun as kids!"

I realized now that God had brought me here so that I would remember the joyful experiences of my childhood that I had forgotten about. God's presence was always with me even in the worst of times.

While meditating later that night, I felt such deep joy permeate and radiate from every cell of my entire being. Turning my attention to Divine Mother, I thought, "Thank you, my Infinite Beloved, for showing me that your joy has always been within me if I had only searched deep within." Tears welled up in my eyes contemplating how much God loves me. I began singing softly to myself Yoganada's chant, "From joy I came, for joy I live, in sacred joy I melt again."

CHAPTER II

Meeting the Guru

God, I want to feel your love,
I am drowning in a sea of maya
looking everywhere for human love
only to be rejected by many egos.

How can I or any mortal love unconditionally?
Yet human love seems so much nearer,
my body can feel the touch
and hear the tender words of another.

Why can't I feel your caress
and hear your compassionate voice?
Please dear God, let me feel your love.

Wrap your infinite arms around me
and rock me gently to sleep,
to remain forever in your samadhi.

Driving into the parking lot at Fort Mason in San Francisco, I thought to myself that I really need to be more spiritually focused like I was in Atlanta if I were ever going to be happy in this life. I pondered that, while studying the teachings of a saint like Yogananda helped me, I felt frustrated that I wasn't alive during his life to receive direct guidance. As I searched for my friend, Lynn, outside of the large meeting hall overlooking the bay, I thought to myself, "Here I go again looking for another spiritual teacher who I think can give me happiness. I thought that when I moved to the Yogananda community, I would live there for the rest of my life... and now I'm discontented again... I feel exhausted from the long drive and lack of sleep. If I can't find Lynn right now, I'm just going to leave... I'm so sick and tired of looking for happiness from someone else.... What could another teacher possibly do to help me that the others couldn't?"

Just as I turned around to get back in my car, I saw Lynn's smiling face as she rushed up to the door to greet me. We sat down on the hard floor toward the back of the sparsely populated crowd. I sat on the women's side of the room talking about inconsequential, worldly subjects instead of preparing for the entrance of a manifestation of the Divine Mother of the Universe. I was asked by a host to move and sit on the men's side. I tried to ignore their rules and moved to the middle of the room so that my friend and I could continue chatting.

Ammachi meets each soul where they are, and gives them a gift from God that is perfect and unique for their spiritual development. When I first met Mother in June of 1988, I actually thought I knew something about the spiritual path. I have been continually astounded by the degree of my ignorance and immaturity in spiritual matters.

I had a standard spiritual question in my mind that I thought of asking this Indian lady. I made it a practice to ask many spiritual teachers how I can calm my mind in meditation. However, I was told by a *devotee* of Amma who was sitting next to me that I couldn't ask her any questions during the evening *darshan* (audience with a holy person), only during the morning programs. I reacted in a defensive manner and thought to myself, "Who cares?"

Amma entering the darshan hall.

Suddenly, I saw people begin gravitating to the rear of the hall and as I turned around I saw a most angelic-looking, smiling, dark-skinned lady dressed in a white sari. I was struck by her luminous visage as I rose to get a better view. After listening to Amma sing inspiring, yet strange-sounding devotional songs, I immediately got in line to be blessed by this cheerful woman. While waiting in line, I felt badly that I couldn't ask this delightful teacher a question. I knelt down to receive a hug from Ammachi who was seated in a chair. As I lay my head on her lap, I was deeply touched by her warmth and unconditional love.

After Mother blessed me, I started walking away but Swami Amritasvarupananda, her translator, shouted to me, "Wait, wait, Mother says you have a question for her!" Surprised that she would know this, I hesitantly asked Amma how I could concentrate in meditation. Mother responded, "Use your imagination that you are lying on the lap of the Divine Mother, then you will concentrate." She then added, "Mother knows that you know this, she is just reminding you. Relinquish all thoughts of me, mine, and I and you will be submerged in the Divine. Mother knows that you know this, she is just reminding you."

During that first crucial darshan, Mother met me right at my bloated ego to capture her son's heart. She repeated that I knew these spiritual truths but that she was just reminding me. I felt rather important that a holy teacher told me that I knew something about spirituality. By reading my thoughts, Mother had let me realize her omnipresence and her greatness. I thought, "Gee, I like her; she's a nice lady."

"In the beginning stages attachment to the guru's external form is good but the disciple should not observe the guru's actions and try to judge him or her. In most cases the disciple becomes too attached to the guru's external form and forgets about his all-pervasive nature."

I'm continually astonished how Mother knows the thoughts of all her children and remembers everyone whom she sees. I went to a retreat with Amma in Northern California in 1988 and got blessed the first evening along with hundreds of devotees. After darshan, Mother walked around the room blessing and touching the devotees who had not been blessed earlier. When I pushed up close to her for a possible second blessing, she looked at me and said in perfect English, "What, you again?" Mother speaks Malayalam, the language of Kerala state in India, and usually one of the *swamis* interprets for her. However, once in awhile Mother will speak in English.

On another occasion, my friend Mary did not get a chance to see Mother until she was in the Bay Area for eight days and Amma exclaimed as she received Mary in darshan, "Eight days, where were you?"

Another friend, Bob, had seen Mother only once several years earlier at the time he and his fiancee were traveling in India. They stopped at Mother's *ashram* (spiritual community) in Vallickavu and when they went up together for darshan, Amma said to Bob, "I've seen you before but not your girlfriend."

Mother can tune her omnipresent consciousness anywhere since the entire universe is within her. She has the ability to speak different languages if she chooses. According to Swamini Amrita Prana (Ammachi's personal attendant), a woman from Yugoslavia came to India to see Amma a few years ago. She was devastated emotionally since she had lost her husband and family during her country's recent civil war. She told Swamini Amrita Prana that due to the language barrier, she was afraid that she would have difficulty communicating with Ammachi.

When the woman went up for her first darshan, Amma began gently singing to her and suddenly the new devotee burst into tears. Later, the woman told Swamini that Amma sang an old Yugoslavian folk song that she had not heard since her childhood! The words of the song were "Be happy, the world is as insubstantial as a dream, so don't let life make you sad." The elated woman returned to her homeland a few weeks later saturated with Amma's peace.

"Surrender leads one to peace and bliss."

From that first evening that I met Mother, she was continually in my dreams for six nights. I became scared that she was taking over my body so I consciously pushed her away. During the retreat in 1988, I told Mother how I got scared and pushed her out of my thoughts and dreams. Expecting the loving Mother who had bolstered my ego the previous week, I was surprised by her response. Amma answered, "If you push Mother away, it is like going to a well and putting water in a bucket and then poking holes in the bottom letting all the water spill out. All your spiritual pursuits are for naught if you push Mother away. You must ruthlessly reject every negative thought. For your spiritual growth throughout your life's journey, accept only good thoughts."

I came away from that last California darshan determined to be positive and not let any negative thoughts penetrate my mind. However, only a few days after I returned home, I felt myself regressing back into a detrimental thought pattern. Without Amma's physical presence, I didn't feel that she was really with me or that she could really help me. Finally, feeling desperate and frustrated one night, I fell in front of my altar crying out with all my heart, "Amma, Amma, I can't stop the negative thoughts. Help me, help me." I then prayerfully repeated for several hours, "Amma, give me peace of mind." All of the sudden, the idea popped into my head to buy a book entitled "How to Heal Your Life" by Louise Hay. I had heard of the book but was not familiar with its contents. The book is about how to heal your life by using positive affirmations.

I rushed to my local bookstore the next day and purchased a copy of the book. After reading the book, I began to understand that the mind is like a tape recorder, how every thought I think and every word I speak is instantly played back. I realized that if I changed the tape in my mind then my beliefs, attitudes, feelings and actions would be different. I then observed that when I became upset with others, my reactions had nothing to do with anyone else's behavior.

I remembered an incident when I became furious at a female friend of mine who began screaming at another person.

This angry woman reminded me of my biological mother. However, another man in the same room reacted differently by saying that he thought it was funny that someone would act like that. That man had a very loving mother, so he responded in a calm and centered fashion. I then began to monitor my reactions and realized that when I became upset at someone it had nothing to do with the other person. I understood that I must vigilantly watch the defective tape that is within me instead of blaming others.

I slowly began taking some responsibility for my actions instead of automatically blaming someone else for my unhappiness. However, I found myself proudly announcing that my anger had nothing to do with the person I appeared to be mad at while I subtly continued to be critical. I would astutely proclaim how a passive-aggressive or hostile person is simply replaying their parent's experience while I was totally oblivious to my hypocritical and deleterious pattern of mimicking my mom's condemning behavior.

A few weeks after I read "How to Heal Your Life," I realized that I really needed Mother's help again if I wanted to stop this insidious blaming tape. A few hours after I wrote a letter to Mother, I suddenly felt a sense of peace flowing through me as my obsessive mind finally slowed down. I understood that even when I appear to act responsibly by telling people that it is me that feels badly about their behavior, I am still blaming them by subtly pointing out their inappropriate actions. Later that day in meditation, I realized that I needed to pray to Amma to give me the strength to empathize with other people's pain, rather than just focusing on how I feel hurt just because someone isn't behaving in the manner that I like. I also needed to be the observer and remain detached from taking things so personally. With Ammachi's Divine intervention, I made a commitment to eradicate my blaming tape by carefully watching my thoughts at the deepest level while trying to reflect how difficult things must be for others.

The detached, reflective behavior and the positive, life-affirming affirmations that I began to use daily helped me to change my negative thought process. I started repeating affirmations that contradicted my judgmental behavior. As soon as I began feeling Amma's love in my heart and started loving and approving of myself and treating others with empathy, I found that my critical tendency began disappearing.

I realized that Divine Mother is never far away when I pray to her with deep devotion. Through daily practice of the affirmations, I was pleasantly surprised that some of my long standing negative habits could be replaced by new, good habits simply by concentrating in the opposite direction. My mind had been filled with pessimistic habits for so long, I realized that it would take a lot of patience, determination and awareness to focus the mind's attention on the positive. Whenever I repeat a *mantra* or an affirmation frequently, I feel more inner peace in my life. However, my ego is desperately fighting to keep the mind focused on the negative to be in control. Ironically, it is when the ego dissolves that the soul will merge into a peaceful, blissful state. It seems that my real battle is not so much with "those harmful people out there" but with the destructive, egoistic part of me that is within.

"Wherever they go, *sadhaks* (spiritual seekers) should either repeat their mantra silently or meditate. Children, through words, character can be changed. If ordinary words can change the character, then think what power a mantra which emanated from the ancient sages can have."

During the first year that I met Mother, a lot of people were asking for mantras. In my immature, spiritual state of mind, I wanted a mantra too, mainly because everyone else was getting one. However, Mother knew that I wasn't ready yet for such an initiation. Even though she told me on several occasions that there was no need for a mantra, I kept bugging her for one. Finally one night during Devi Bhava, Mother asked me who my favorite deity was and I told her that I followed the teachings of Paramahansa Yogananda. Mother, in her omniscience, responded, "Yogananda worshipped the Divine Mother so just worship the Divine Mother." I finally realized that she wasn't going to give me a mantra and so I let go of the idea of receiving one. However, one day several years later, I had an intuitive feeling that it was all right for me to ask for a mantra during a Devi Bhava program. When Amma finally whispered the sacred words into my left ear that night, my entire body shook with the thrill of receiving the initiation. I feel that I have cherished and used the mantra more often, after trying unsuccessfully to obtain one for years.

**"In olden days, marriage was not only considered
as a physical union of a man and a woman
but as an oath taken by both, a joint endeavor
to help each other lead a righteous life with
God-Realization as the ultimate goal."**

Mother responds differently to each soul who comes to her based on each person's *vasanas* (latent tendencies). Like the ancient Indian healing system of *Ayurveda*, what may be good for one constitution could be harmful to another.

I asked Mother during the first year if I should get married or be a *brahmacharya* (celibate spiritual aspirant). She said that marriage is a lifetime commitment so it's better for me not to get married. However, a woman I know asked Mother to pray for her that she may find her soulmate and get married. Mother said that she would pray for her and the woman met someone and got married within a year.

**"Obedience to the guru's words is the
only way to cross over all obstacles which
arise in the spiritual path."**

I have asked Mother questions at times to obtain the results I wanted to hear rather than following her advice. Whenever I have followed my ego rather than Mother's advice, I have gotten into trouble. In fact, there's one sad incident when Mother told a man not to leave the ashram in India because he was going through a difficult astrological period. However, he ignored

Mother's words and left the ashram, subsequently meeting with a fatal accident.

During the second year that I saw Amma in 1989, I foolishly asked her the same question about marriage hoping for a different response instead of listening to and accepting her advice given the previous year. This time she responded emphatically, "It would be a disaster if you got married." I then asked her if I should become a monk and she responded, "You're not mature enough to be a monk." Since I seemed to be on quite a roll, batting a thousand, I figured I'd ask her one more question. Therefore, I asked her if I could move into the new M.A. Center ashram in San Ramon and she replied, "It's not up to Mother; it's up to the board of directors."

She knew I wasn't ready for ashram life and she really had to teach me quite a few lessons to help me grow up emotionally and spiritually. Mother has frequently told the devotees that a *mahatma* (a great soul) is like a doctor who may have to squeeze the pus out of a wound which momentarily creates pain, but the treatment results in the patient being healed. Finally, I understood Mother's message about moving into the ashram. Amma, you are the board of directors of the Universe who has been molding this pathetic piece of clay; kneading me more as I am needing you more.

"Bowing down to all of existence is a state of total acceptance, you stop fighting with the situations that arise in your life. You fight and struggle only when you have an ego, only when

**you are identified with the body. When you shake
off the shackles of the ego, no more fighting is
possible. You can only accept."**

Since Mother knows what's best for everyone's physical and
emotional state, she gives advice according to each person's constitution. In Ayurveda, I would be classified as a *pitta-vata* (fire
and air). Unfortunately, my *dosha* (constitution) is very sensitive
and can get out of balance easily. Therefore, when I asked Mother
for advice on how I could stay healthy, she responded, "Do not
forsake sleep and get plenty of rest." During the first retreat at
the San Ramon ashram, I was very tired and didn't feel well. I
knew I wouldn't get much sleep if I stayed at the ashram so I
decided to spend the night at a nearby cheap motel.

I felt guilty and ashamed for leaving the program to get a
good night's sleep because I thought all the other devotees were
staying in the ashram doing *tapas* (austerities). However, the next
day when I sheepishly went up for darshan, Mother looked directly at me and spontaneously said, "You can stay inside the
ashram or outside, whichever you prefer." I'm always judging
myself that what I'm doing is never good enough, yet the great
saints always accept each individual where they are.

**"If one puts his heart and soul into an activity,
it will be transformed into a tremendous
source of inspiration."**

In the early years of Amma's visits to the United States, she
used to frequently dance after giving darshan. At the end of one

morning program at the San Ramon temple, she began dancing wildly as the chanting became louder and louder. All of the sudden, she stopped dancing and collapsed on the floor in a state of

Mother in a blissful state.

samadhi (state of absorption into God). It was thrilling to see Mother merge into the Divine state. After several minutes, she stood up and ran to a waiting car. It appeared that she was trying to remain in body consciousness by tapping herself on her head. As she entered the car, her body collapsed again into a state of samadhi. Experiencing a glimpse of Amma in the Divine state reminded me of the Yogananda chant: "What lightening flash glimmers in Thy face, Mother! What lightening flash glimmers in Thy face! Seeing Thee, I am thrilled through and through! Seeing Thee I am thrilled through and through!"

"Unless jealousy within is removed God will not come before us."

During the 1989 tour, a lot of the devotees noticed that Amma was giving a lot of attention to one boy in particular. She saw that some of the devotees were becoming jealous. In her infinite compassion, Amma explained to the envious devotees that the reason why she was spending so much time with one boy was because his mother died when he was a baby, and he always asked his dad why he didn't have a mother.

"One who has sincere love for God will see His form everywhere."

Amma, a great mahatma, is one with all of creation and sees no differences between various souls. However, some people who visit Amma from different spiritual paths have been criticized by members of the same spiritual organization for spending time with a saint who is from a different tradition. Mother had said that some devotees who judge people for seeing Amma have never experienced the bliss of being with an *enlightened* master and that they sometimes forget that the disciple is supposed to see the guru and Divine Mother everywhere and let go of "me and mine." A spiritual teacher once told me that if you put all the masters in one room they would agree on everything but if you put all their disciples in one room they would agree on nothing. I have found that it is important for me to follow my inner guidance as I search for God rather than acquiescing to whatever unenlightened people say I "should" be doing. The search for God is very personal and unique to each soul and only a truly realized master can guide one to the goal.

"Any action performed without discrimination is *adharma,* an unrighteous act. You need absolute discrimination to know and understand the difference between what is good for your spiritual progress and what will create obstacles in your path."

Amma frequently encourages us to use discrimination when making decisions instead of telling us what to do. I once asked Amma about finding a spiritual environment to live in, and her response was, "Mother will pray for you but you have to also spend time looking. You should use discrimination in whatever you do, and Mother will always be with you." In other words, if I am using discrimination and putting out the positive energy, I will be guided by God rather than my little ego.

For many years I had a desire to visit India and I had asked Mother about making a trip there. I asked her, hoping that she would take away problems that have happened to me on previous long distance trips. My constitution is thrown off balance when I travel and the vata imbalance causes illness and nervousness. I told Amma about the problems and concerns I had about making such a trip. Mother's response was, "It is best not to go to India until the difficulties are resolved."

However, I was determined to visit Amma in India in October 1990 and I chose to ignore any possible difficulties that could arise during such a pilgrimage. My poor judgment and impulsive behavior created quite a few complications for me. When I landed in Madras, I was overwhelmed by culture shock. I stayed in a noisy, dirty, cheap hotel where all my senses felt assaulted. Indian Airlines was on strike and I couldn't fly to Mother's ashram. I became physically ill and decided not to continue on to Amma's ashram. I felt sad and embarrassed that I traveled all the way to India but did not make it to her ashram.

At the time that I met Ammachi, I considered myself a devotee of Parmahansa Yogananda. I decided to visit spiritual sites near Madras and to spend more money on better hotel accommodations. When I arrived at the new hotel, I was pleasantly surprised to see hanging by the lobby the exact picture of Yogananda that I had on my altar. Very few of the 800 million Indians had heard of Yogananda and he was especially unknown in South India. I felt it was a Divine blessing to have that picture greet me and after seeing that positive sign, the rest of the trip became quite enjoyable. As I meditated at the *mahasamadhi mandir* (a holy site of a saint's conscious exit from the body into God union) of Sri Aurobindo in Pondicherry, I felt my soul merge into his Divine light and love. Wave after wave of bliss encircled my body as I experienced deeper and deeper states of inner peace.

Although the trip was a disappointment on one level, I felt that God was guiding me spiritually throughout the pilgrimage. The spiritual experiences continued as I landed in Los Angeles; here I went to visit the ashram where Yogananda had lived. I sat outside the large white building wondering if I would be able to meditate inside his room since the building was temporarily closed for repairs. Suddenly I heard Yogananda's booming voice clearly shouting, "Don't worry about getting into my room, you should be concerned with letting me into your room (heart)." After the thrill of hearing his voice, I felt inspired to chant a Yogananda song entitled "Door of my heart, open wide I keep for You." When I've opened my heart to God regardless of the outer circumstances, the Divine truly manifests.

A month later I had another special experience on the grounds of the Yogananda ashram. In 1980 I spent a few weeks in Morelia, Mexico, studying Spanish. While there, I met a young student, Sandra, who was interested in practicing her English. We had corresponded throughout the years and I sent her Spanish copies of both *The Autobiography of a Yogi* (Yogananda's autobiography) and Amma's biography. I visited Sandy in Los Angeles in November of 1990 and we visited the ashram. As we walked along the beautifully manicured green lawns and colorful rose bushes, Sandra suddenly began shaking and said she had the chills. I couldn't understand why she would be cold since it was a warm, sunny day. Sandy explained that one of the most significant dreams she ever had in her life happened the night before she met me. She dreamt that she was walking with a man dressed in white with dark, curly hair and a mustache in a spiritual setting in front of a three story white building. She suddenly recognized that I was the man in the dream as we stood in front of the building that was Yogananda's home. Everything that happened in her dream ten years earlier was occurring before her very eyes at that moment.

"Death is only a change like all other changes. This change of the body has nothing to do with the soul which will remain unchanged as ever. All those who have taken birth will die. But death for knowers of God is something different. They are not afraid of death. Instead, they will welcome death. They do not enter the world of death. They enter the world of God."

After completing my spiritual pilgrimage in Los Angeles, I returned home to Nevada City. A good friend of mine, Paul, had been very ill with cancer for six months prior to my trip to India. When Amma was in San Ramon in June of 1990, I showed her a picture of Paul and she asked Swamiji (Amritasvarupananda) to write him a note stating "My darling son, you should see everything as coming from God. Mother is always with you. Kisses and hugs, Amma." When I brought the letter to Paul, tears welled up in his eyes as he lay helpless in his hospital bed. He was dumbfounded that a great saint would bother to write him such a personal note and he hoarsely whispered, "She wrote this to me?"

Over the last six months, I had been one of Paul's primary caregivers and was concerned that he had taken a turn for the worse right before I left for India. As soon as I returned home, I called the hospice home where he was staying, only to discover that he was dying and that I should come right over.

When I entered Paul's room, I was shocked to see his emaciated body as he lay mute and paralyzed on a neatly-made hospital bed. Light was pouring through the large picture window and the room was filled with a fragrant aroma from the many vases of flowers. Paul was a disciple of Yogananda so I reached into my wallet and held up a picture of Yogananda's last smile (the picture that was taken of Yogananda as he left his body and went into Mahasamadhi in 1952).

I beheld Paul's brown eyes squinting to see the photograph more clearly. I gently murmured to him, "That's good, Paul, go into Yoganada's light." As his pain-wracked, virtually lifeless body lay dying, I noticed a slight smile appear on his face as his eyes focused deeply on Yogananda's form. As his soul began to merge deeper into the Divine light, I sang to him the words from the Yogananda song "From joy I came, for joy I live, in sacred joy I melt again." After a few minutes I felt it was time to leave the room. I bent down and hugged him good-bye as I whispered into his ear "Go into Yogananda's Light; go into God's Love. May God always bless you dear friend." Right after I left the room, he fell unconscious and died the following morning.

I felt that it was God's grace that by returning early to America, I was able to help my friend during his transition to the other side. When I have chosen to see obstacles as opportunities, even my seemingly inauspicious visit to India manifested some spiritually uplifting experiences for me. Perhaps Divine Mother knows when my intent has been pure so that even when I have suffered physically and emotionally, the spiritual rewards have been great.

CHAPTER III

Darshans in San Ramon

Oh Lord, what can I do?
Oh Lord, where can I turn?
Oh Lord, I'm so lost without Thee,
Where in the world can I know the truth?

"Look within your heart, my child."

**A man in India in 1982 who used poor judgment
came to Mother for forgiveness:**

**"The guru's compassion forgives all. Seeing the
helpless man's condition, Amma could not help
but allow her motherly compassion to overflow.
'How can Amma curse you or punish you? She can
do neither. How can a mother even dream of doing
such a thing? Don't cry.' Amma hugged the young
man, wiped his tears, put him on her lap and
rubbed his back with compassion and love."**

I have been under the illusion that I actually decided
when I was going to spend time with Mother. However,
Amma has said that she calls her children to come see
her at exactly the right time in their life. She has also said that

all of her devotees have been with her in a past life. After traveling to India and not making it to her ashram, I felt too embarrassed to visit the San Ramon ashram during the rest of the year. As a defense mechanism to cover up my shame for not seeing Mother in India, I tried distancing myself from her by diving deeply into worldly pursuits.

Instead of accepting and expressing my feelings of humiliation about not visiting Mother, I totally tuned Amma out of my life after the India trip. I came up with an extensive list of excuses why I didn't have time to see Amma during her two weeks in the Bay Area the following summer in 1991. "Coincidentally," I had to be in the Bay Area on the evening of Mother's first darshan in San Ramon so I figured I would just stop by to check out the scene. As I drove onto the ashram grounds, I arrogantly thought to myself, "Look at all those funny-looking people, many of them dressed in white. It kind of reminds me of a Klan meeting. Those people standing in front of that temple look like a bunch of groupies waiting for a rock star to appear... I have nothing in common with those weirdoes. If they could only see how ridiculous they look to a normal person. I wonder if they're going to start selling their books in airports."

I stood at a distance from the temple, observing what I thought to be the inane excitement of the crowd. Someone spotted Mother walking down the hill from the main house and shouted, "Mother's coming, Mother's coming." I contemptuously mimicked what I saw as religious fanaticism by whispering in a sarcastic and disrespectful tone to myself, "Mother's coming, Mother's coming; big deal." As Amma walked by and the throng pressed in closer to get a glimpse of her, I sardonically thought to myself, "Look at the robots doing the latest dance; the guru prance." I acerbically laughed at the automatons who couldn't even think for themselves, instead playing follow the leader. Standing at the back of the hall with my arms folded tightly against my chest, I figured, what the heck, since I'm already here, I might as well go up for darshan and get some chocolate. (After Mother blesses the devotees by hugging them, she gives them a chocolate kiss and flower petals) "Anyway I'm hungry and really love chocolate."

I became quite frustrated that the line took so long, wishing she would hurry up and more quickly bless those mindless idiots. Whenever I saw someone enter from the side who didn't have to wait in line, I became furious at those pushy people. I almost got up to tell one obese woman who was shoving her way to the front, blocking my view, that she should get in line like everyone else. Who the heck does she think she is anyway? However, I was slightly embarrassed when I realized that she probably had cancer as she took off her hat to show Amma pain that she was experiencing on her bald head. I still sat there, oblivious to Mother's compassion and the uplifting singing, just thinking about dining at that new Thai restaurant with my friends once I left San Ramon.

As I became fifth in the darshan line in front of Mother, suddenly I started shaking and crying uncontrollably. Unexpectedly, a wave of Divine bliss blew through my being like a zephyr flowing through a field of lilies. I felt deep remorse for having closed my heart to God and behaving in an arrogant, condescending manner toward the embodiment of the Divine Mother and her devotees. Through my tear-stained face, I begged the Holy Mother for forgiveness for my transgressions. When I finally went up to receive darshan, Amma gave me the most accepting glance, letting me know that everything was all right. She then gave me a mesmerizing and enchanting look of compassion when I told her that I went to India but did not make it to her ashram. No matter how many times I've turned away from the Divine, God has always forgiven me. What else can a Mother do?

"Nothing is impossible for a Mahatma."

Now that I was finally back in tune with the Holy Mother, I tried to be as open as possible to receive her Divine grace since, God only knows, after the way I behaved, I surely needed it. At the end of the week, I had a sweet and captivating experience of the Holy Mother's compassion and omnipresence. The chant "He Amba" [pronouned "Hey Amba"] was sung frequently during the 1990 tour and one of the devotees wrote down the notes for me to play the chant on the *harmonium* (an organ-like keyboard instrument with small metal reeds). I really enjoyed playing this inspiring chant to God in the form of the Divine Mother. However, after spending one week listening to *bhajans* (devotional singing), I hadn't heard my favorite song "He Amba" performed.

As I stepped outside of the San Ramon Temple, I asked one of the Indian brahmacharyas why they hadn't played the chant. He was busy and simply replied that it's up to Mother when various songs are played. I then said to myself, "Oh well, I guess I need to give up attachment to hearing that particular song." As I reentered the temple, to my amazement, the Holy Mother gazed in my direction and began singing "He Amba." During the evening program, I told a devotee sitting next to me what had transpired earlier in the day. My eyes were closed as I deeply tuned into Mother singing "He Amba" again later that night.

Amma singing to the Divine Mother.

As I sat in front of the Holy Mother in deep meditation, her form disappeared as she metamorphosed into pure translucent light. The light grew brighter and brighter encompassing the entire universe. I then visualized how lying on her lap earlier that day, I was hugging a solid person who was at the same time the source of universal energy. When she blessed me that morning on the spiritual eye between the eyebrows, my entire body shook as if thousands of volts of electricity soared through my nervous system. I cried out, "Oh Mataji (Mother), Oh Guruji" as surges of bliss radiated up my astral spine (located two inches in front of the physical spine). As the song came to a close that evening, I slowly came out of a deep meditative state. The devotee sitting next to me said, "Your eyes were closed but when Mother sang 'He Amba,' she looked at you and smiled."

Amma, being one with all creation, can manifest her Divine energy anywhere in the world in any form she chooses. I asked her during the last darshan how I could really be certain that her Sacred essence is truly with me. Amma responded, "Don't worry, Mother is always with you." However, I replied that it's difficult for me to really believe this.

When I returned home from my visit with Mother in the Bay Area, I attended a service at the spiritual community where I used to reside. I noticed that it was strange that the same incense (natural fragrance) that permeates Mother was being burned in the community temple that morning. Later that day, I mentioned to a friend how unusual it was that Ammachi's incense was being burned at the temple and my friend responded that incense wasn't being burned during the service. Although I was sure I smelled the fragrance, I began to wonder if the odor was just a manifestation of my active imagination. However, a few hours later I went to a meeting at a public school. As I entered the room, I smelled Amma's delicate rose fragrance again. Astounded, I kept walking around the door sniffing the delectable scent of the Holy Mother while several people looked at me strangely. I knew that this was no figment of my imagination. "Ah, Amma is truly with me!"

I also experienced that Mother is with my soul whether I'm awake or asleep. A friend of mine suggested that I may be interested in hosting a foreign exchange student since I enjoyed foreign cultures and children. I contacted a foreign exchange student organization and after an interview, I was told that they had a student from Thailand who could stay with me. The only thing I knew about Thai geography was that Bangkok is the largest city. However, that night I had a dream where I saw a town 120 miles northwest of Bangkok and suddenly Amma flew over the town. A few days later when I received the information on the exchange student, I found out that Tone (the foreign student) was from a small town 120 miles northwest of Bangkok. A few months later Tone arrived and spent a year with me studying in the United States. I learned a great deal from his Buddhist philosophy and he in turn absorbed a lot of Mother's teachings, finally meeting her in person.

"If he so wishes, a *Satguru* (Realized Spiritual Master) can even bestow *Self-Realization* (the state of complete identity with the Higher Self/God) on his

**disciple or devotee. He can do anything he likes.
His will is one with God's will."**

The goal of devotees on an Eastern spiritual path is to reach *moksha* (Self-Realization), to get off the cycle of death and rebirth so that we can eternally melt into God's Light. I learned during Mother's visit that nothing can compare to receiving the grace of a realized master in achieving this goal. A friend of mine had been very depressed because his wife had died a few months earlier due to a chronic debilitating disease. He and his wife had spent a lot of time with Mother during her first two visits to the United States. When he discussed the passing of his wife with Amma, she said that due to his prayers and Mother's will, his wife has no more karma to work out and will not have to be reborn. Although on an emotional level he still grieved for his wife, he was grateful that through Mother's grace, her soul is free, merged into God's Infinite joy.

In a similar circumstance, a Western man who visited Amma in India was extremely distraught at the sudden death of his gentle four-year-old boy. As Mother tenderly held the grief-stricken man in her arms, she told him that the boy was a very advanced soul who only had a few lessons to learn in the body and now has merged into God forever.

**"Spirituality can be experienced only in
stillness and silence. Energy will be wasted if
you speak. Be careful when you utter a word. One's
life span, health and vitality are
decreased through talking."**

I tend to use talking as a defense to be in control so I won't get hurt (the best defense is a good offense). I have noticed that most of my useless chatter is done just to bolster my ego.... "Look at me and see how great I am. Hey, will you approve of me now? Not yet, well how about this bit of information... and this... and that"...ad nauseam....

During the San Ramon retreat in 1991, I volunteered to do *seva* (selfless service) by cutting vegetables for dinner. I was being my usual unconscious self, talking away about frivolous items, when Mother walked out onto the deck where I was mindlessly chopping chard. She unexpectedly came up to me and took the knife and vegetables out of my hand and showed me how to prop- erly cut the greens. As she rolled the chard into an impeccable snake-like form, I beheld perfection with each chop of the knife. As Amma skillfully cut the greens, she looked directly into my eyes and said, "Mantra, mantra, mantra." Through God's grace, I was fortunate to be directly taught by a great mahatma that even cutting vegetables needs to be done with total concentra- tion, in silence, as a service to God.

"Hard work is needed to make even a small crack in a big solid ego. Try to point a finger at someone's ego and expose how identified he is with his ego. He will erupt like a volcano, and the lava of protests will start flowing. He reacts out of total identification with his ego. How can people like this realize the truth about their ignorance?"

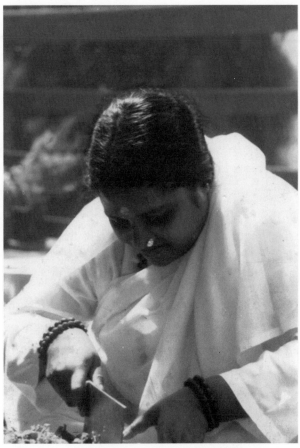

Amma cutting vegetables.

Opportunities for learning spiritual lessons seem to develop intrinsically whenever I'm in Mother's physical presence. She certainly did a job par excellence in chipping away at my hardened ego during one *satsang* (spiritual gathering) in Palo Alto in 1992. At the beginning of morning darshan, I noticed that there was no one on the men's side of the darshan line directing traffic (called the lap person) as the devotees approached Mother. I suddenly got this bright idea to ask one of the satsang leaders if I could help out by being the lap person on the men's side. I was filled with excitement. I felt proud at pulling off this "coup d'etat" of having the best seat in the house, and also having people think that I had an important job in helping Ammachi.

However, when I was informed that I could be the lap person that morning, I had an inner feeling that the job would be a disaster. After fifteen minutes of cheerfully encouraging the devotees to move up in line, Mother angrily shook her finger at me as the translator stated, "Mother wants you to let the children and older people come up first from the line on the side." I then enthusiastically began letting all the children and older folks come up to Amma. About ten minutes later, Mother vehemently shook her arm as the translator declared, "Amma says if you just let the people on the side up for darshan, the devotees waiting in the center line will get upset." I then created an ingenious plan to let every other person in on both lines while developing an elabo-rate exit space. Moments later as I looked up, I saw Amma furi-ously shaking her finger at me again and I was told loudly in no uncertain terms, "Mother says she'll tell people when to come up; you don't know how to do anything."

At that point, I just wanted to evaporate into the floor but sat still, paralyzed full of fear and embarrassment for the rest of the satsang, not moving a muscle. After that harrowing experi-ence, I decided I needed to receive a loving embrace from Amma and decided to go up for darshan once everyone had been blessed. Mother usually whispers sweetly into the devotees ears as they lay in ecstasy on her Divine lap, "Ma Ma, Ma," (Divine Mother) or "My son, my son, my son." Expecting these melodic words emanating from Amma, I was rather taken aback when I heard a loud and stern "No, no, no, no, no!"

After that ego-crushing experience, I reacted with trepidation when I was asked to be in charge of supervising the salad preparation for the retreat dinner on the weekend. Although I told the head cook that it may not be good for me to be in charge, I was still assigned the task. However, I judiciously visualized a scenario that if Mother could see me supervising and cutting the vegetables properly when she returned to the house after the morning satsang, she would think that I wasn't such an egotistical maniac.

I wanted to do an impeccable job. A retreatant, who was a professional cook, told me to put some broccoli in the salad bowl but since I was the supervisor, I was sure that the broccoli wasn't supposed to be included. I left the room to check with the head cook. Of course, I was wrong. When I returned to the kitchen, I beheld Amma standing right at my cutting board smiling and touching all the vegetable cutters. However, as soon as I came closer to "my" station, she turned around and walked away.

The next morning, I asked one of the Indians how to say "I love you" in Malayalam (the language of Kerala state in India). The man wrote down "Amma ye Jhan sneyhickannu." I thought I would redeem myself by doing something special, speaking to Ammachi in her native tongue. When I went up for darshan, I said in probably the most horrendously pronounced Malayalam, "Amma I love you". I had no idea what actual words came out in

Malayalam but Amma began laughing uproariously telling Swamiji, the translator, how funny I sounded. When the laughter subsided, Swamiji replied, "Mother says she loves you too."

"Fear results when people are tossed about by their own petty desires, always concerned only about themselves. A true master is constantly in meditation, even though you may see him being physically active. His presence is the most conducive place for your Self-unfolding to take place. In his presence you can attain that inner aloneness and thereby get rid of all your fears and feelings of otherness."

Fear of being physically and emotionally hurt seems to be what has been motivating my behavior throughout my life. In 1992, I was asked to pour out the oil from the lamps that were used after a Devi *puja* (the worship ceremony that takes place before Devi Bhava) and in my fear that I would not get a good seat close to Amma afterwards, I worked too quickly, ending up spilling oil that I had collected all over the floor. I then became afraid that if I didn't go for dinner at the beginning of Devi Bhava, there would be no food left for me later in the evening. As soon as I cleaned up the oil spill, I ran to the food line. However, I noticed that two hours later there was still plenty of delicious food left for everyone.

In response to questions I had about my fears a few days later, Amma said, "You need to have a deep awareness and faith that Mother is always with you. Be courageous, Mother is always protecting you." I then pleaded with Ammachi to let me know that she's truly with me so I won't have anything to fear. When I sat down to meditate after receiving darshan, I felt her radiant bliss manifest in my spiritual eye. I beheld an iridescent golden circle of light enveloping another ring filled with a shimmering azure color and at the very center was a glimmering silver star. My soul was drawn toward the center of that majestic light. In that profound state of absorption in the Divine, all my fears dissolved.

**A resident in Ammachi's ashram in India stated:
"Mother removed my illness so quickly
one day. A few moments later the same
symptoms were seen in Mother. Yet in
Mother it lasted only a few minutes."**

At the end of the first week of satsang with Mother in 1992, I became quite ill. During Devi Bhava darshan, I prayed deeply that she would heal me and I drank several glasses of holy water (Amma blesses water during the Devi puja ceremony). However, upon arising the next morning, I felt worse and I was literally too weak to get out of bed. With a foolish lack of patience and faith, I began doubting Amma's ability to heal anyone even though I had watched the "Vintage Scenes" video in which Mother actually healed a leper's wounds by licking his skin.

As I lay in bed feeling angry and disgusted, I sarcastically thought to myself that yesterday I drank a lot of holy water and prayed deeply to Amma to heal me and this is the result? However, in the early afternoon the thought popped into my head that I should see an acupuncturist. I looked in the phone book and the only one in the area was all booked up. Luckily, the acupuncturist decided to arrange a special time to see me. The session greatly improved my energy level to the point where I was well enough to continue seeing Mother in the Bay Area. As I was leaving the acupuncturist's office, I noticed a jar of chocolate kisses and rose petals on the receptionist's counter; the exact items Mother gives her children during darshan!

Amma seems to come to me in various forms when I pray to her with deep sincerity. However, sometimes Mother chooses not to heal devotees so that they will progress spiritually. I have learned that illness can be considered an opportunity for me to pray deeply to Amma with all the strength of my heart. I remember that Amma wrote to my friend Paul who was dying of cancer that we should see all things as coming from God.

Mother's omniscient nature makes her the ultimate Divine physician who can perfectly diagnose and heal any illness. I asked Amma why I have had problems with illness and with falling asleep. She told me that it is due to excessive heat in my body which confirmed the diagnosis of high pitta I received from an ayurvedic doctor. She told me that I should get a sandalwood stick and make a paste out of it and apply it to my forehead every night. As I calmly fell asleep that night after applying sandalwood paste, I felt as if my body was bathed in Amma's peaceful aura.

A friend of mine was in a serious automobile accident and consequently was experiencing severe headaches. A neurologist wanted to operate on him, which would have been quite dangerous and a very expensive surgery. Mother told him that the operation was not necessary and within months the headaches went away. However, Amma is also very practical, recommending that many devotees follow the treatment of their doctors, either allopathic or ayurvedic.

"Various names and forms are meant only to help us in our spiritual practice."

In 1992 I was inspired to ask Mother for a spiritual name. I felt that I was asking for a new name because I wanted to deepen my spiritual connection with Amma rather than making the request to simply bolster my ego. Sweat was pouring down my brow as I nervously approached the Holy Mother for my new name. I was afraid that she may give me a bizarre sounding name or one that had an uncomplimentary meaning. Swamiji wrote down my new name: "Dayalu", meaning the compassionate one.

The following day when I was in the question line, I said my new name to Swamiji and he was concerned that I mispronounced it and stated, "It is Da 'ya' lu with the accent on the 'ya'." He then turned to Mother to tell her that I didn't know how to say my new name correctly. Mother smiled at me and patted my head repeating, "Dayalu, Dayalu, Dayalu." Although I was embarrassed that I couldn't even pronounce my name correctly, my inadequate verbal skills resulted in a delightful experience with Amma.

I liked the sound of the name and enjoyed the fact that it meant "Mr. Nice Guy". However, it wasn't until a few years later that one of the Swamis told me that Amma sometimes gives names in order to develop qualities that you may be lacking. The Swami joked with a smile, "Now, Dayalu, don't get angry, remember you are the compassionate one."

"You can speak about spirituality for hours in very beautiful and flowery language, but still spirituality will remain unknown to you unless you really experience its beauty and bliss from within."

During Devi Bhava, a few days later, I truly experienced Mother's bliss and grace. After receiving darshan from Ammachi, I sat down behind her to meditate for a few moments. I've always had a difficult time concentrating while meditating. My monkey mind constantly jumps from one topic to another. However, when I sat down to meditate that night, I suddenly felt waves of ecstasy flowing through my entire body; molten currents of light and peace like nothing I had ever experienced! I was transported into another dimension beyond time and space. My attachment to the body evaporated as I felt myself merging with a universal power of indescribable love and peace. The only thought I remember having was that this must be what being on "cloud nine" feels like.

I felt Divine Mother's energy entering and transforming all of my chakras. I couldn't move my body or open my eyes. I bathed

Amma blessing Dayalu during Devi Bhava.

in Mother's luminous light for an indeterminate amount of time. Unfortunately, I became afraid that I was losing control and in a desperate attempt to assert "authority," my lower-self decided it was time to descend back into limited body consciousness. However, I was still transfixed in a Divine state and couldn't move, which only created more fear. Finally, after much effort, "I" was finally able to open my eyes and a few minutes later, I slowly and unsteadily arose and staggered off the stage. I then had to rest on the floor for a few minutes to get grounded. I wondered to myself how I could drive home in this state, drunk with Mother's Divine ambrosia.

As I safely floated home that night, inebriated in her infinite love and light, I became aware that the inner battle lines were drawn between the ego, desperately fighting for its limited self-centered life, and the all-encompassing peace and joy of Mother's Divine light. I prayed to Mother *Kali*, "I am a bubble; let me merge into thy sea."

"Just as the mother hen protects the little ones under her wings, a perfect master always protects the aspirant."

Besides constantly uplifting the devotees' souls, Mother is always protecting her children. At the end of the 1992 program in San Ramon, a close friend of mine, Shakti, experienced Mother's grace in a rather dramatic way. In the early morning of the last day of programs in the Bay Area, Amma was pacing back and forth stating that something bad was going to happen to one of her children that day.

The final program at the San Ramon ashram had ended and the devotees were breaking down the temple in preparation for packing things up and traveling to Los Angeles. Shakti climbed an old extension ladder to take down a banner that was hanging from the top of the ceiling which was about three stories high. The ladder was not completely secure on the slippery floor and slid out from underneath him. Suddenly, he fell thirty feet, landing on his head and arm when he hit the concrete floor far below. One horrified observer remembered that she could literally see his head bouncing off the cement. The shocked devotees in the temple came running toward him fearing the worst. A nurse happened to be nearby and she was surprised that he was still conscious. He was rushed to the hospital by the paramedics but miraculously only suffered a broken arm.

Shakti later described the accident as if Amma had put an invisible net beneath him to break the fall. However, karmically he still had to go through the experience. The Holy Mother later told him that astrologically he was destined to die that day but through Divine grace, he survived. Amma said that the Universal Mother had absorbed his karma that day and what would have been certain death became a minor accident. The banner that Shakti was taking down was a symbol of "*Sri Chakra*" which represents the Universal Mother. This was the last thing he grabbed onto for support as he began plummeting toward the concrete floor.

In another dramatic incident, an American devotee was recently traveling from Singapore to India to see Mother when her plane developed mechanical problems. The aircraft suddenly dropped 25,000 feet, diving toward the Indian ocean. Just at that exact moment in India, Amma mentioned that a devotee's plane was shaking a lot, and she casually inquired which devotees were on the plane. At the precise moment when Mother tuned into the disciples whose lives were in danger, the aircraft regained its momentum and was able to safely return to Singapore.

One Indian disciple erroneously told Mother that the plane had crashed. However, Amma replied, " The plane did not crash. My devotees were on board." Later, when the devotee arrived at the ashram and immediately went up for darshan, Mother told everyone, "Her plane had been shaking a lot and had dropped."

Recently, three ashram residents were driving down the very steep, curvy road from the San Ramon's East ashram at night. A rabbit suddenly scurried across the road. The driver swerved to the left, hitting her brakes. The car veered off the road and the vehicle was precariously lodged above a gully located hundreds of feet be-low. As the driver and passengers crawled out, the car swayed back and forth almost toppling over.

I was asked to pull the car out with the tractor. One of the passengers, Dharman, had hooked the chain to an opening at the bottom of the car and wrapped it around the front loader using the headlights from the tractor. He then entered the wobbly vehicle, shifted it into neutral and released the emergency brake. I prayed deeply to Amma to help us out of this dangerous predicament. As I backed up, the chain broke off from the car and the vehicle was thrust forward toward the creek hundreds of feet below. My heart skipped a beat as I saw Dharman desperately trying to stop the car. With Mother's grace, the car skidded a few feet then came to an abrupt stop. Hours later, a tow truck driver carefully dragged the car up the ravine with a winch. The next morning when I visited the site of the accident, I was surprised to see that there was no foliage to have stopped the car and after observing the sixty degree angle of the tire tracks, I could not understand how the car didn't flip over. Amma, Amma, Amma!

"Children, this Ashram is not Amma's. This place exists for the world."

Unfortunately, Ammachi is only in the Bay Area for a few weeks during the year. When Mother leaves, I feel devastated and sorrow-ful at the thought of waiting an entire year to spend only a brief time bathing in her love. Since I lived three hours away from Mother's ashram until 1995, I had difficulty feeling her Divine presence in the "real" world. I wish I were more of an advanced soul to be able to tune into her no matter where I am. When I have been with Mother I was filled with energy and joy, yet when I returned home, I frequently felt my contentment slowly slipping away.

Paramahansa Yogananda frequently wrote that environment is stronger than will and that it's important to associate with like-minded seekers to continue growing spiritually. Unfortunately, not everyone can live and work in a spiritually uplifting environment. I know that devotees are supposed to feel God's presence within, since realistically we can't always physically be with our spiritual teacher. However, I have found it quite arduous to be constantly aware of God when dealing with difficult work situations, my inevitable emotional and physical problems, and with family and friends.

The main way I have stayed in tune with Amma during the year had been by making pilgrimages to Amma's ashram in the Bay Area. In 1992, I decided to spend three or four days each month at the M.A. (Mata Amritanandamayi, Mother of Immortal Bliss— Mother's formal name) Center in San Ramon. As soon as I would drive onto the ashram land, I felt a sense of peace envelop me. When a great avatar (incarnation of God) like Mother lives for two weeks every year in an *ashram*, she permeates the land with her Holy vibration.

The regular evening programs at the ashram are spiritually uplifting with either a talk or a reading and bhajans. While more devotees attend the Saturday night programs, each and every satsang is filled with Mother's spiritual energy. During those visits to the ashram, as soon as the bhajans began, I would usually feel a great energy rising within me and my body would start pulsating with

Divine bliss. I would close my eyes and feel Mother's presence within. Upon opening my eyes, I would be surprised not to see her physical body sitting in front of me, as her joy permeated every cell of my body. Jesus said that when two or more are gathered in His name, he is present. In the same way Mother comes to her children as the devotees sing devotional songs together.

M.A. Center in San Ramon, California.

Besides experiencing the joy of tuning into Ammachi's presence during the morning chanting of the names of Divine Mother and evening programs, I have come to understand the benefit of performing selfless service. When I stayed home on weekends trying to figure out how to satisfy my sense desires by going to the movies, eating out at restaurants or visiting with friends, it seemed that frequently my energy level was low. The more I engaged in recreational activities for myself, the more I needed to keep fulfilling one insatiable desire after another, which only created a deeper and deeper sense of alienation and emptiness in my life. However, when I stayed at the ashram performing seva, I was surprised that I was full of energy and contentment.

I've noticed that when I wanted recognition for what a good job I did performing seva, I wasn't as fulfilled as when I dedicated my work toward God. Sometimes when I've done a task around my house mindlessly I would feel exhausted, yet when I've remembered to dedicate the work to God, my energy level would increase. Perhaps this is the difference between doing work for one's lower self versus selfless service.

"The guru instructs the disciple in which path he should choose and gives advice according to his character or nature. The sole intention is to reach the goal."

After Mother left the Bay Area in the summer of 1992, I wanted to ask her if I should move to Albuquerque to study Ayurveda. I had a friend ask Mother the question in Rhode Island. Amma responded, "It would not be best for his spiritual growth if he moved there." I felt incredibly blessed that I have a living master who can omnisciently see my soul and guide my spirit to its highest goal.

Many months later, I had another friend take a note to Mother in India that simply asked whether I should go see Mother in India. With hundreds of people asking Mother personal questions daily, her individualized response really surprised me. She replied, "You can't go wrong if you're going to see Mother. He didn't have to write Mother about this. It's not like when he asked about moving to Albuquerque. He had to ask that because he did not know if it was for his highest spiritual growth. I think he'll understand what I'm referring to." Only the Divine manifesting in a physical body could have a memory like Ammachi.

CHAPTER IV

My First U.S. Tour

Remember... remember... Divine Mother... Divine Mother,
Let me see Thee,
Everywhere, ...in everyone ...in everything...

Remember... remember... Divine Mother... Divine Mother...
Let me see Thee
in all my thoughts... in all my fears...
in all my dreams.

"What you should give up is the attachment to the object. You can have the object and enjoy it if you are not attached. We give up something externally, in order to be internally free from the bondage to that object. Detachment is what brings peace and happiness."

While being motivated to go on Ammachi's 1993 US tour, I still had some reservations about making such a long spiritual journey. The ego came up with all sorts of fears and concerns. When I arrived at the airport in Seattle to greet Mother for the first leg of the journey, I was surprised to see hundreds of people there to welcome her. I felt very nervous as I waited for her arrival. However, as Mother entered the huge international receiving room, I felt myself becoming peaceful and calm. Right after Mother hugged me, I noticed that an astrological gem (worn to counteract the negative influences of a planet), a small green peridot that I had been wearing for a year and a half, was missing. I thought that it was very strange that the ring that I had worn for so long that wasn't even loose, disappeared right after I greeted Mother. I asked Amma what happened to the jewel the next day at the Seattle retreat. Mother told me, "Once the negative effects of a planet have been nullified, the gem sometimes disappears since it's not needed anymore. Don't worry about it." Although I had frantically searched all over the airport for the gem, I realized that it wasn't a coincidence that it vanished right after greeting Amma.

**Mother told one of her devotees in India:
"Son, how will you get grace as long as you think 'I am doing?' On the contrary, you do not have the attitude of surrender characterized by the feeling that 'I have offered everything to Divine Mother, Divine Mother will save me.'"**

One evening at dinner during the Seattle retreat, I sat next to one of the devotees who asked me if I had ever done any acting. At first I replied not really but then "I" got excited when I heard he was looking for someone to be in a play that he wrote that would be presented in front of Mother and hundreds of devotees. Then I realized that this would perhaps be the ultimate test of breaking down my inflated ego by making a fool out of myself in front of Amma, and I became scared. I only agreed to be in the play when Mother said it was all right. I had a great deal of fear and anxiety about acting in the performance. I was petrified that I would forget my lines while standing on the stage in front of everyone. As the day of the play drew closer, my anxiety level increased. I kept thinking that I would look like such a complete idiot as I forgot my lines, spoiling the play for everyone in the cast and audience.

As I anxiously stood in the wings ready to go on-stage the night of the performance, I unexpectedly became calmer and calmer as if I had just entered a deep state of meditation. As I entered the stage in this peaceful state, I kept mentally repeating Amma's name. The play went off without a hitch for all the actors and throughout the performance. When I have performed in other plays, I would become so nervous that I would break out in a cold sweat and my knees would literally shake. However, with Mother's grace, I've seen how she can transform anxiety into inner peace. If she can alter my emotions in a brief skit, I can hardly imagine what great changes she can bestow upon this little character in the larger *leela* (Divine play) of life.

"What is received through guru's grace is God's grace."

During the darshans this year, I experienced on a deep level that Mother is not really confined to her body. When meditating in front of her, I had an incandescent vision of how the entire universe is contained in this little five- foot lady clothed in a plain white sari. Her body metamorphosed into a transformer of Divine light with a multitude of planets and stars revolving around her.

Sometimes Mother transforms her children without their knowledge, on both the gross and subtle levels. For some strange reason during the past year, I found myself spontaneously and frequently saying the word "*Shiva*" out loud, regardless if I were alone or with other people. Shiva is the Hindu Deity who is the destroyer of the ego, allowing us to merge into God's love. Amma and her devotees greet each other with the mantra "Om Namah Shivayah" which means "I bow to God within you." I asked Mother about repeating the name "Shiva" and she turned to me with a surprised look on her face and responded, "It's a good sign that you are saying Shiva." Mother played her part in this leela impeccably as she acted astonished when I told what happened. However, I knew that she was really the one who planted the name in my consciousness.

For a few months prior to seeing Amma that year, I was intrigued with the idea of going to a facility where I had heard of a healer who was supposed to help one release traumatic experiences from past lives. In the new age movement when there are so many people doing various healing techniques, it's difficult to know which modality can really help. I was surprised with Amma's response about my possibly visiting the "past lives" institute. She said, "It's best not to go. Only a Mahatma can take away negative past life experiences." I'm slowly learning that the search for inner peace and God-Realization can only be guided by one who is enlightened.

"Children, you are all dreaming and you believe that the dream is real. No amount of explanations can make it clear to you. Until you wake up, and for as long as you identify with the dream, it will remain unclear. Wake up and you will realize that you were only dreaming, and then everything will become clearer than the clearest."

On the way back from the retreat at Fort Flagler to Seattle, my friends and I took a late morning ferry. I assumed I would see Mother next at the evening program in Seattle. My friend's six year old son, Aaron, saw a video game on board that he wanted to play. After I showed Aaron how to play the game, I also became mesmerized, trying to manipulate a yellow face to eat as many black dots as possible. I barely heard my friend, Esther, in the background yell " Dayalu, look!" I really didn't want to be bothered to stop playing the game since I had a good chance of beating my previous high score. I screamed back at her while concentrating on winning the game, "What's so important?"

Just as I yelled toward Esther, I saw Mother walking by out of the corner of my eye. Was it a vision? No way! I immediately hurried to follow Mother onto the upper deck. As I ran after the Holy Mother, I thought to myself, "What a metaphor for my life. I'm always getting so involved in illusory games that I'm not able to notice Divine Mother when she walks right by me." However, when I finally awakened from the video dream, I received quite a blessing, standing next to her on the deck of the ferry as she gazed out on the majestic bay and forest singing to God. At one point Amma froze, enraptured in samadhi, merging

Amma on the ferry to Seattle.

into the Divine surrounded by radiant Mother Nature. Her eyes developed a far-away look as if she were gazing into other celestial worlds as she resumed her chanting to God at the end of the boat ride.

As the ferry ride came to a glorious finale, Amma departed the misty outdoor deck and entered the video room. She had seen Aaron and me playing video games earlier so she walked right up to the different flickering amusement signs. Some of the devotees were embarrassed to notice that most of the games were quite violent. One man remarked that the games are like the battle between darkness and light at *Kurukshetra* (famous battle scene from the Indian scripture Bhagavad Gita). I put some quarters in the game that I had been playing and Amma, in her child-like innocence, joyfully played with the strange American buttons that made the smiling yellow face eat up the black dots. I thought to myself, "Amma's eating up all our vasanas so we can merge into God forever and won't have to come back again and again to play a never ending series of video games. Without Amma's grace, we would be stuck in *maya* (illusion) like Sisyphus endlessly pushing a boulder up a hill."

Mother discussed a recent incident that happened at the ashram: "That calf was a *sannyasin* (a renunciate monk) in its previous birth. Due to its karma it took birth as a cow. Because of the accumulated merits from its previous birth, it happened to be born in this ashram. The brahmacharins

**raised it. It grew up hearing the Divine Names.
This way it left its body."**

During one darshan in the Bay Area in 1993, I asked Mother
to pray for my sweet dog, Shalom, who was my faithful companion for sixteen years and had died six years earlier.

While waiting in the darshan line, I remembered that cold,
lonely February morning in 1971 when I decided to get a dog
after I had just returned from living for six months in Israel.
Upon my relocation to New Jersey the previous month, I found
out that my childhood dog had died while I was gone. Feeling
depressed and needy, I went to the local dog pound searching for
the perfect replacement pet, but all of the dogs looked so pathetic I just wanted to leave. However, on the way out, I noticed
a little black mutt with brown spots and floppy ears who was to
eventually become a source of unconditional love for me. For
sixteen years I anthropomorphically treated this animal as my
best friend. "Shalom" became my trusted companion and play-
mate through nine changes of residence and as many relationships. At times I felt embarrassed that I had such a deep love and
concern for a mere animal.

God's grace had saved my dog's life on several occasions.
Once when Shalom was an arthritic fourteen-year-old, my friend,
Nandita, suggested that I let the dog off the leash so she could
move freely in the woods while we were hiking. However, Shalom slipped as we strolled near the edge of a cliff. I was horrified
as I watched my dear companion plummeting hundreds of feet
down to a rocky valley toward what appeared to be her certain

death. I forged my way down the cliff as fast as I could contemplating how I would transport her body to a veterinarian as soon as possible if she were still alive. When I arrived at the bottom of the hill, to my delight, I saw Shalom standing in a shallow creek between two gigantic boulders. She had miraculously landed uninjured in the murky water.

A few months later, when I had just moved to the Yogananda community in Northern California, Shalom suddenly came down with a serious disease that caused her to keep falling down or walk in circles. Some people told me to let her die but I wasn't ready to let go of her. I prayed and even demanded that Divine Mother allow her to live another year. Sadly, I drove her limp body to the local vet where my beloved canine was put on an I.V. and given large dosages of medication. Through God's grace, Shalom slowly recovered from her illness and although a little worse for wear, she was still able to enjoy life and continue playing her role as my loyal companion.

However, two and a half years later when Shalom was sixteen, she finally became too sick to eat or walk. I knew that it was time to take her to the vet to be "put to sleep." With constant praying to Divine Mother, the journey to the vet went easier for me than I expected. Approximately an hour after the dog left her body, I sat down to meditate and suddenly saw a bright light and beheld Shalom's essence looking for me. She appeared confused so I held her astral body which felt as real as her physical one and began stroking her. I kept mentally telling her to go into the light. After some time the vision slowly faded. Two hours later when I meditated again, I saw Shalom running back and forth very quickly, barking like she did when she was a puppy. She was bursting with energy and joy being able to run around, free of her old garment of a dilapidated body. My dog would sprint toward me and then abruptly return back to the other side.

Although I felt blessed to find out Shalom was "alive" and well on the other side, I still had to mourn for the loss of my long-time friend. I had put a picture of her on my altar the day she died and had been praying for her soul. However, after a few days, while meditating, her picture suddenly fell on the floor face down. That seemed to indicate to me that it was time to really let go of her.

I remembered that during my grieving stage, I had called an erudite spiritual teacher who was a long time member of the Yogananda organization in Los Angeles. After counseling me, he mentioned that a member of his congregation had lost a dog and two months later another dog had appeared on her doorstep. I thanked him for the advice but told him that I really didn't want another pet. However, exactly two months after Shalom died, I moved into a new house and there was a friendly, black hound waiting for me on the doorstep whom I named Karma.

Now as I approached Ammachi in the darshan line, I felt embarrassed to ask such a great Mahatma such a trivial question as, "Would she pray for my deceased dog who left her body six years ago?" I had hoped that Mother would simply respond that she would pray for the dog's soul in the astral plane. However, her answer really surprised me. Ammachi replied, "She is now a

My dog Shalom.

girl almost five years old and will become a devotee, a strong believer in God in her life!"

Mother wouldn't say where this little girl was living. How incredible that my puppy dog that I'd been mourning for is really a five year old girl. If my dog was now really a five year old child, then there truly is no death! What a great example of maya! For years I was sad about missing Shalom when in reality she was a little girl, possibly even residing in my neighborhood! It was good that I didn't find out where she was currently living because I'm sure the parents would have been horrified if I showed them pictures of what their cute girl looked like a few years earlier, or worse yet, if they had seen me walking their "daughter" on a leash in the neighborhood!

"Children, a pure *sankalpa* (resolve) has great power, but only when the sankalpa is pure will it bear fruit."

The same day that I asked Amma about the fate of my dog's soul, I asked her why I'm not shaking anymore when I get blessed during darshan. For five years whenever Mother touched my spiritual eye or blessed me, my nervous system became electrified and my body would shake uncontrollably. It felt like an electric current was pulsating through me. Ammachi responded, "Mother made a sankalpa that the shaking would become more internal. Eventually the energy will become pure bliss." She then added, "You've become more mature." She looked deeply into my eyes and said "Om Namah Shivayah."

If I have matured at all it is only due to Mother's sankalpa because, left to myself, I would never evolve. How compassionate that Amma made a sankalpa without my even asking her, to help my spiritual growth. I've learned that if I keep opening my heart to the Divine, I will receive God's grace.

"A living *satguru* is absolutely necessary to guide the aspirant during the course of his sadhana. Following a spiritual path without a guru can be compared to sailing alone in the ocean in a tiny boat that is not equipped with the necessary equipment, not even a compass to indicate the direction."

Mother patiently helped me with some spiritual confusion I was experiencing. I had been following the teachings of Paramahansa Yogananda for many years prior to meeting her, yet felt so drawn to being with Amma. In her cogent and expansive manner, Amma told me, "Yogananda is the father aspect and Amma is your Mother for eternity."

Yogananda entered mahasamadhi (a saint's conscious exit from the body) in 1952 and the method I had been employing to seek his spiritual wisdom was reading books and meditating on his form. Unfortunately, I have found it has been easy to delude myself in the absence of the physical presence of an enlightened spiritual teacher. I have noticed that when I have a desire, even though I have "meditated" on how to do God's will, frequently the answer I have received in meditation has been my ego's wish under the guise of "God's will."

Many, if not most, spiritual seekers worship a deceased spiritual master, whether it be Jesus, Buddha or Ramakrishna. One may reach the goal of union with the Divine through sincere devotion, such as Saint Francis impeccably following the teachings of Christ. However, in my particular case, I feel I really need to have a living master to guide me.

By 1993 I had been living in a spiritual community based on Yogananda's teachings for almost 10 years. I was unsure if I should spend more time in Mother's ashram in the Bay Area or remain on the Yogananda path. I prayed intensely as I approached Mother with this important question. However, as I meditated in the question line, I felt Yogananda's presence clearly and heard his booming voice urge me, "Go to Divine Mother, go to Divine Mother, go to Divine Mother."

When I asked Mother the question, she told me, "If you want to worship Mother more, you should live in her ashram." To make the transition easier for me, she added, "If it doesn't work out here (in San Ramon), you could always go back to the other ashram." That night I had a dream where the current president of the Yogananda center in Los Angeles came and blessed me.

Later, I received further confirmation of following Amma's spiritual path when on the way to her Los Angeles retreat, I stopped at Yogananda's crypt at Forest Lawn Cemetery to meditate. As I became deeply absorbed in meditation, Mother's unmistakable rose-scented fragrance filled the mausoleum. I felt a deep sense of inner peace through this Divine resolution to my conflict.

"The love of a Mahatma is beyond words. The love that you see and experience outwardly is of course deep and intense, but that depth and intensity is only an infinitesimal fraction of what he or she really is which is infinite."

Mother has been teaching me to experience her from within rather than only focusing on her outward form. Whenever Mother enters or leaves the darshan hall, most people run after her trying to receive another blessing. One day I rushed in front of the crowd and knelt next to the door as

Mother put her sandals on to leave the hall. She then walked right smack into me. Bump! Thud! She immediately touched my leg and then herself in the Indian style of apology. I was mortified that I was so unaware as to get in the way of the Holy Mother, causing her an accident. However, one devotee told me that it was no accident that Amma bumped into me and that whenever one is touched by a great saint it is considered quite auspicious. After that traumatic experience I tended to stay behind the crowd and tried to feel Mother's energy from within, rather than focusing on her outward form.

The previous year, I had one of the deepest spiritual experiences of my life during Devi Bhava right after darshan. I then believed that I needed her physical touch in order to achieve another deep ethereal experience. While waiting in line during Devi Bhava in San Ramon 1993, I sat down on a chair in the audience about 75 feet from Mother.

All of the sudden I felt my crown chakra open up as I felt a profound Divine energy penetrate my entire being. I was transfixed into a state of bliss, unable to move or talk. When this joyful state finally subsided, I tried to go up on the stage for darshan but I was so intoxicated with Divine Mother's love, I could barely move. It was difficult to open my eyes and when I finally received darshan, I realized I didn't need to constantly receive Amma's personal touch to feel the formless aspect of the Divine.

When I arrived in Chicago, I had five questions to ask Mother for myself as well as for three other people. I wanted all of the inquiries answered that morning so I wouldn't have to keep asking questions during the rest of the tour. As soon as the darshan began, I sat next to Swamiji who said that Mother wasn't answering questions that morning but he asked me to remain seated just in case she decided to answer. Mother let me sit next to her for two hours before she responded. It really surprised me how she answered each query in detail, and in perfect order, after such a long pause.

It was very hot and humid in the basement auditorium where the Devi Bhava darshan was held. I received a clear inner message not to go up for a blessing due to the heat and crowds. I sat in front of a huge fan in deep meditation feeling cool, calm and peaceful. Through God's grace, I now realize that at times I have the capacity to feel Amma's Divine presence within.

"A mother will be naturally loving and compassionate towards her children and will look after their needs."

Like a biological mother, Amma continually makes herself available to help her children. In 1993 I was on a flight with Ammachi from Chicago to New York. There was a middle-aged woman devotee who was exhibiting a great deal of anxiety about flying. Mother compassionately asked the nervous lady to sit right behind her and arranged for Swamiji to sit next to the woman even though they weren't able to get much sleep the night before due to Devi Bhava ending after four a.m.

I noticed Amma spent a long time in the bathroom upon entering the plane. When she came out of the rest room, Mother appeared to be in a blissful state of samadhi. The meal cart was blocking the aisle but Mother simply accepted the predicament, standing in the back of the plane until someone directed her into a seat. As the aircraft climbed toward its cruising altitude, I went into the bathroom and noticed that a rose-scented fragrance permeated the room. That toilet turned out to be a great meditation spot as I soared higher and higher in Amma's vibrations. When I came out of the bathroom, Mother happened to look up from her seat and gazed deeply into my eyes. She put her hand on her heart as a smile lit up her face and she said, "Om Namah Shivayah." We touched our hearts and looked deeply into each other's eyes for a special moment in eternity.

"As the child grows, the feeling of insecurity will also grow, as he discovers that being with his parents is not real security. The parents who are in the world are foster parents. We are God's children. The Lord alone is always with us."

Upon arriving in New York City, I dreaded facing a difficult family situation. My mom was deteriorating rapidly with Alzheimer's disease. When I visited my parents' New Jersey home, my mom thought that I was still in high school and that the family dog who died twenty-three years earlier was barking in the basement. She behaved in a bizarre, rude and enraged manner. Needless to say, my father, who had recently undergone triple bypass surgery, was at his wits end not knowing how to cope with this horrendous situation.

In spite of my elderly parent's horrific physical and emo-
tional condition, I was able to bring them to be blessed by Amma.
My mom became quite confused as we entered the crowded
Manhattan church. I held her withered hand and guided my oc-

My parents visiting me in California.

togenarian father toward the light of God. With some difficulty,
my dad slowly knelt down at the feet of the Holy Mother while
my disoriented mom kept inquiring in a childish manner what
she was supposed to do next. As I helped my dad up, I brought
my mom closer toward Amma's radiant form. Suddenly my
mom became terrified and claustrophobic surrounded by so
many people and refused to go any closer to Ammachi. My
mom stood frozen in a state of fear and confusion.

Amma quickly got up out of her chair and began rubbing my mom's heart chakra. The light of God began to gradually penetrate her hysterical and frightened soul. A large smile slowly spread over my mom's face as she began whispering to Amma, "Thank you so much , thank you , thank you, thank you." My mom's countenance became filled with peace and delight like a little girl who was being comforted by her mother's love. My mom's biological mother died when she was seven years old and she had been angry her entire life because she never had a mother to love her while she was growing up. Finally at the end of her life, she was able to briefly experience what she so craved for eighty years: the unconditional love from the Divine Mother.

Amma then called my dad forward as she blessed this elderly couple's union by showering them with flower petals for their final few months of a fifty-three year old marriage. As I led the rose-petal-covered ancient couple from the church, one devotee remarked, "Both your parents are glowing; they look just like newlyweds."

My Dad has described himself as an agnostic in spite of his commitment to Judaism. While feeling awkward with the foreign cultural milieu of Amma's program, he said he was touched by her kindness and love. My dad had been complaining of severe pain in his hip before he received darshan. As we left the New York church, I told him to apply some of the holy ash that Amma gave him to his hip. The following day, I told my dad how Amma is one with the Divine and has extraordinary healing powers. He turned toward me sheepishly and said that he was embarrassed to tell anyone but that after he put the holy ash on his hip the previous night, the pain went away.

Although bringing my parents to Amma to receive her blessings was spectacular, the trip to New Jersey brought up a lot of old childhood emotional pain. At the satsang a few days later in Boston, I prayed to Amma inwardly to help me deal with the emotional distress that was restimulated by the visit. I cried out inwardly, "Oh Amma, you're my only hope, my only salvation. I feel as if I now have no parents. I am a lost orphan without your maternal guidance. Please help me Amma. I am so alone in the world without your love and compassion guiding me to my true home."

I asked Mother to pray for me when I went up for darshan. When I told her of the difficult situation with my emotionally disturbed mom, she wisely replied, "You need to understand that her problems are due to old age and she's not really angry at you." Ammachi, an ever flowing river of compassion, added, "Amma is your mother now." As she looked at me with deep affection, I felt the muscles in my body relax as all my tension and anxiety dissolved into her light. A feeling arose within me that Amma has entered my heart for eternity and I didn't really need to keep desperately looking to friends and relatives for love anymore. As I meditated that evening, I thought of the Yogananda chant "No birth, no death, no caste have I; father, mother have I none; I am He (one with God), I am He, blessed Spirit I am He."

"Perform your duties without thinking of past experiences, future expectations or the fruit of your actions. Always live in the present, doing your duties as a service to the Supreme."

As I have opened up more and more to Mother, I have been able to release the past and live more in the present. Ammachi has said that the past is like a canceled check. Sometimes I wonder why in my case the checks keep bouncing. However, I did experience Amma's grace when I visited my old, red brick, three story junior high school in New Jersey during the tour. As I stood in the sweltering heat meditating on the building that was once a source of enormous pain, I felt agonizing memories suddenly evaporate as if I were watching a movie of a past incarnation.

I experienced suffering as an early adolescent by not being accepted by my peers because I lacked athletic prowess at the time. I prayed to Mother to release me from the entrapment of my past emotional trauma as I entered the antiquated institution of learning. A sunbeam was shining on a huge poster as I entered the dark and dingy gymnasium. I noticed a magnificent portrait of Mahatma Gandhi tacked on the green paint-chipped wall stating "Strength does not come from physical capacity but from an indomitable will." I suddenly felt a sense of completion as I read my junior high school's message from an Indian saint proclaiming the importance of inner rather than outer strength.

"Where there is surrender there is love and compassion, whereas fear results in hatred and enmity. Surrender means welcoming and accepting everything without the least feeling of sorrow or disappointment."

Mother wanted the play that we performed in California changed in order to include more spiritual teachings. I had a week to learn many new lines and by the time I arrived at the final retreat in Rhode Island, I felt confident that I could recite the new script by heart. However, Mother always seems to push her children to their limit to help us expand and grow spiritually. I was informed on the day before the play was to be performed that Mother wanted even more spiritual teachings added.

I obstinately opposed memorizing the new lengthy dialogue because I felt that a great deal of the added verbiage could be eliminated while still communicating Amma's teachings. However, the real reason I resisted was because I was afraid that I would forget my lines. My life would be so much more peaceful if I always just accepted everything as coming from God. I didn't sleep well the night before the play and was too exhausted to adequately learn the new lines. I spent most of the day in a fog, in a futile attempt at memorizing words which became nebulous, so that I wouldn't make a fool out of myself in front of Amma and the more than six hundred people in attendance at the evening program.

As I walked on the stage that evening, I realized that only Divine grace could save me from imminent disaster. To minimize the embarrassment of making a complete idiot out of myself, I asked another devotee to prompt me if I forgot my lines. However, I forgot to tell the actor, who was hidden behind a bush prop, that prompting consists of only whispering the first few words of a line.

As I stood speechless on the elevated stage with hundreds of people as well as the Holy Mother staring at me, the prompter, who happened to be from England, began loudly reading a five line monologue in a proper British accent. I quickly thought to myself that maybe I should act like a ventriloquist and pantomime the speech but who would believe my newly found English accent? However, as all the actors stood helplessly staring at the talking bush, one thespian became agitated and started yelling at the prompter, "Shut up, it's not helping him any."

Suddenly, another actor interrupted the prompter by skipping to the next scene and we resumed the part of the play that I could have recited in my sleep. To my amazement, even when I was standing on stage looking like a blithering idiot, not knowing what to say, I felt a sense of calmness. It was as if Mother and I were totally alone in the huge gymnasium trying to figure out

Actors with Amma after the play (Dayalu is standing behind Amma).

how to get through this terrifying ordeal. Through Mother's grace, the faux pas was hardly noticed and everyone still enjoyed the production. When I have held on tightly to Mother's lotus feet during difficult challenges, I have realized that nothing can really harm me.

"Spiritual power is always radiating from a Mahatma which certainly creates spiritual energy in us when we sit in his presence."

When I'm with Mother, I feel like I'm plugged into a Divine generator. Usually I get tired easily when I travel with a lack of sleep but when I'm with Amma I find that she keeps me full of her infinite spiritual energy.

However, when I'm not in Amma's presence, my energy level drops and time goes by so slowly and I long to be with her. Yet in the longing of wanting to be with the Holy Mother, I feel that I am becoming closer and closer to the Infinite Beloved.

I noticed that when I'm in Mother's vibration, I feel her spiritual power manifest in myriad ways. At the end of the retreat, I needed to drive through three states and by as many airports to catch my flight at Newark air terminal. I wanted to share a ride in my rental car with another devotee but never got around to asking if anyone else needed a ride to New Jersey. Most of the retreatants were flying out of Boston. However, as I was leaving the retreat, serendipitously I met someone who needed a ride to Newark and whose plane was leaving at the exact same time as mine.

"The mind will merge in the Supreme State through constant practice and all our efforts will bear fruit."

A few months after I saw Mother in Rhode Island, I attended a retreat at the ashram in San Ramon. The devotees were blessed to have one of Mother's main Swamis from India, Swami Ramakrishnananda, lead the three-day retreat. The weekend program was structured with the devotees meditating for eight hours each day, singing bhajans, and engaging in other spiritual practices. Swami Ramakrishnananda told the devotees that Mother would be with us in spirit, since she could not physically attend the retreat. He also said that if we put forth the effort, at the end of the retreat we would see the results of our spiritual efforts bear fruit.

Although I forced my hyperactive self to sit quietly during the many hours of daily meditation, my mind was not about to cooperate. Throughout the meditations my mind indulged in all sorts of spiritual pursuits such as contemplating... "if the department of transportation builds another deck on the Bay Bridge the commute time to San Francisco would be reduced; ...since frozen yogurt is fat-free, is it better to buy a small or medium size? ...if I were to unexpectedly meet my old girlfriend, Laura, would I be able to interest her in the spiritual path?"

Besides pondering these profound metaphysical questions, I was also able to make up for some lost sleep as I noticed how quickly the meditations flew by. Although I felt like a complete failure at meditation with my monkey mind jumping from one frivolous thought to another, at least I forced my body to sit quietly. Toward the end of the last meditation, I unexpectedly had a vision of an unfamiliar old Indian man. I have rarely seen a picture of a person while meditating and was enchanted with this startling experience.

When the retreat ended, I was driving on a freeway to my friend Lynn's house in Marin county when suddenly in my mind's eye, I saw the same unidentified elderly man again. When I arrived at Lynn's cottage, which was nestled amongst giant redwood trees, she asked me if I was interested in seeing a spiritual video she had just borrowed that morning. As soon as Lynn turned on the video, I exclaimed, "Oh my God, I just saw that man a few hours earlier while meditating and driving here." The video was about the life of Ramana Maharshi, a great Indian saint. I was deeply touched by his compassionate eyes which elevated me into a deep state of calmness. Swami Ramakrishnananda was so accurate when he said that Mother was with us during the weekend and if we put forth spiritual effort during the retreat, we would receive a boon.

"A parrot raised in a temple will repeat Divine names while one raised in a liquor store will repeat vulgar names."

When I visited the M.A. Center in San Ramon during the year, I felt Amma's sacred presence and experienced much joy. However, when I returned to my rural mountain-top home, I found myself reverting back to a *tamasic* (low energy) life-style. I had been a television addict for most of my life, watching rajasic programs for many hours daily. This behavior was in such contrast to that of blissfully sitting in front of the Holy Mother during the summer as I watched her celestial drama unfold. I knew how detrimental it was for my spiritual and emotional growth to continuously watch low-consciousness shows, but like an addict I couldn't discontinue this downward spiraling motion by my own volition.

The materialistic, superficial characters on television had become a pathetic substitute for uplifting human interactions. I've seen how easily my mind can justify any *adharmic* (non-virtuous) behavior. I desperately tried to rationalize how each insipid show I watched had some redeeming social values: at least the "Leave It To Beaver" reruns illustrate how a loving family should act; I'm increasing my intellectual pursuits by watching "Jeopardy;" viewing "Oprah Winfrey" helps me to have a better understanding of my clients' problems.

One propitious winter night in January of 1994, I was lying bundled up in bed watching a horrific movie about a mass murderer. I finally exclaimed to myself, "This is absolutely crazy to watch this trash." At the end of the movie, I wrote a letter to Amma asking her to help me turn the TV off so I could turn Divine Mother on. Right after I wrote the letter, the idea popped into my head to unplug the antenna from the television. That night I threw away the antenna cord and never watched television again. There's no way that my weak-willed ego could have ever gone cold-turkey by itself, disconnecting the television for good. However, by aligning my will with Mother's omnipresent Divine energy, an entrenched habit was instantaneously dissolved!

CHAPTER V

Beyond Death

Jai Jai Ma
Oh my beloved Lord
Thy love is flowing into my heart
living, loving, dying into thy light.

"An accident occurs due to your careless driving. What foolishness it is if you come out of the car and scold the fuel for creating the accident! Likewise, in our struggle to protect our false pride, we commit all kinds of negative acts."

When I first moved to the rural Sierra mountains in 1984, I used to drive in a frenetic manner, inching up right behind anyone who drove too slowly until they finally pulled over to allow me to pass. After residing in the pastoral countryside for several years, I noticed that my driving had finally slowed down and other cars would flash their bright lights or honk at me to pull over on the narrow, curvy roads.

I was proud of my emotional and spiritual development as I looked disapprovingly at the reckless drivers who needed to impatiently speed to their destination. Watching the bright lights flash into my rear view mirror at night, I shouted to myself at those immature, "Type A" people, "Why don't you grow up and slow down?" Being the epitome of tranquillity and maturity, I decide to teach those inconsiderate drivers a lesson in how to achieve calmness and inner peace by passive-aggressively driving as slowly as possible, which would of course only infuriate the speedy drivers.

On the way to the airport to see Ammachi at her first program in Seattle in May of 1994, there was an accident on the main freeway and I found myself at a stand-still for about forty-five minutes. I thought to myself that I am a calm, spiritual man who is on his way to see the Holy Mother. Will I become anxious about possibly missing my plane, or remain in a meditative state, realizing that Amma will take care of everything? Knowing how much spiritual progress I had attained, I thought to myself "no problem". However, as the traffic situation worsened, I started to become mildly nervous that I would arrive late at the airport. Following the spiritual principles that I'd been so arduously studying, I decided not to leave it all up to Amma, but to use discrimination to meet the challenge.

I expeditiously decided to take a back country road rather than wait in traffic any longer. I began to drive calmly on the curvy road maintaining my spiritual equilibrium by observing my breath and slowly repeating my mantra. However, to my dismay, I found that I was becoming quite lost while taking the short-cut. As my anxiety level increased, I began driving faster and faster, forgetting my mantra and deep breathing techniques. As I became more frantic, I thought to myself, "I don't have time to focus on any stupid mantra; I must get to the airport right now or I'll miss the plane and then what will I do? I might lose the money for the ticket or better yet, have to spend the night at the airport which will cost a fortune. I knew I should have left earlier." I honked my horn at all the stupid, slow drivers in front of me. I cursed those lazy idiots moving at a snail's pace while recklessly passing them on blind curves. "I'm on my way to see Amma, the embodiment of love and compassion, and these dummies are getting in my way!"

While waiting an hour for my plane to take off at the Sacramento airport, I reminisced about my spiritual progress since I met Mother six years earlier. I embarrassingly thought of how hypocritical I had been. I thought, "Even after all these years pursuing a spiritual path, I'm really no different than the wild teenage drivers whom I've been condemning."

"The *jiva* (soul) which makes the body act, departs leaving behind the corpse. Death is not the complete destruction of the body. It is the beginning of the decomposition of the five elements with which the body is made of, only to merge with its original principles. This change of the body has nothing to do with the soul which will remain unchanged as ever."

My biological mother died on December 19, 1993. The death of a parent, regardless of age, is quite an emotional challenge. The person who was supposed to nurture me and give me unconditional love had departed permanently from my life. While the spiritual teachings helped give me comfort and peace, I still had to deal with the feelings of the loss of my mom. Only through God's grace was I able to have the strength to adequately cope with her transition.

I had just returned from spending five glorious days at Amma's ashram in San Ramon when I checked my answering machine a few days before Christmas. I was shocked to hear in the message from my sister, Judy, that my mom died suddenly from an infection since she had been in good physical health. After allowing myself to release sadness, I wiped away the tears from my face and sat down to meditate. While praying deeply, I asked the soul of my mom to go toward the light. Unexpectedly, I felt my mom's presence and it seemed as if she were confused in the astral plane and didn't know where to go. I told her to ask God to help her.

During the meditation the following morning, I asked her soul to go toward Divine Mother's light and love. I felt her responding that she met a beautiful Indian lady with a crown on her head who had comforted her. I visualized kissing her good-bye and telling her I loved her. Later that day when I tuned into my mom's soul during meditation, it appeared as if she were involved in some project dealing with light beams in the astral plane. It seemed that she was already well into her new life just over forty-eight hours after leaving her body.

The next day in meditation, I felt my mom indicating that Divine Mother was in charge of the light beam project she was working on. Her energy seemed different. She was less attached to me and the Earth plane than the day before when I felt her presence in meditation. She said that she forgave everyone who had her hurt her. She added that she had blinders on when she was in the body but that she is not going to hold on to any guilt for the mistakes she made.

I kept saying my mantra during the plane trip back to New Jersey. Although I have had sleep problems when I travel and when I deal with emotional crises, through God's grace, I slept well the night before the funeral. The next morning in meditation, I told my mom that today was the funeral and I felt her reply that her dead body is not her real identity. She added that she has been grateful for all I have done but the funeral is for the people on Earth. She seemed much further away that day and it was harder to make contact with her.

After attending the emotion-packed funeral, I meditated and felt my mom indicating that she witnessed the ceremony but was detached from it. Although she seemed distant, her energy was unusually kind and centered. She seemed to no longer need to be angry all the time like she was on the Earth plane. It felt like she was in the astral plane but also had the ability to observe and be close to the Earth.

On the day after the funeral, I tried contacting her soul, but I felt Amma's presence intervene, telling me that it was distracting her. There was a veil I couldn't and wasn't supposed to penetrate. I felt Ammachi's presence communicating that the love that I miss from my mom is God's love, but that now I would receive the loving energy from my mom without the anger that used to be mixed with it.

When a younger relative told me that he felt no sadness over my mom's death because he felt that she was hostile and rude toward him, I told him to look deeper to find some loving things that she did for him. I felt tears welling up inside me as I told him how I felt her love when she made a special pie crust for me with cinnamon and sugar that I used to enjoy eating. I realized that one of the reasons I chose my mom was to learn the lesson of forgiveness and to be able to see a spark of God's love in all souls, no matter what their outer appearance may be.

Since my mom spent her entire life being angry due to effects of a bad childhood, I thought that she didn't progress spiritually at all in her life. However, when I asked Amma about the passing of my mom in Seattle, she told me, "Your mom released her anger when she left her body and she is exactly where she is supposed to be in the astral plane. She has to come back for a few more births to work some things out." Through Amma's grace she released her rage when she left her body and has been thus able to progress spiritually.

Only the great mahatmas can truly see each soul and I, with my tunnel vision, am unable to understand each being's purpose in life. Amma has helped me to accept everyone exactly where they are. Each soul has different lessons to learn. I used to encourage all my friends and relatives to see Ammachi, but now realize that it may not be the right time in their evolution to become involved in a spiritual path, and that my proselytizing would only create disharmony.

"In most cases the disciple becomes too attached to the guru's external form and forgets about his all-pervasive nature."

When I met Mother at the Seattle airport at the beginning of the 1994 tour, I was surprised that I wasn't as thrilled to see her for the first time. I thought to myself that perhaps Mother had been with me more internally and her physical presence wasn't quite as important. During the first meditation that I attended with Mother at the Fort Flagler retreat, I saw an expansive bridge climbing higher and higher into a crystal-clear azure sky. This gateway opened up to a most majestic light, shining with turquoise, gold and silver. God's light gently touched my heart as I sobbed softly to myself.

After experiencing a peaceful meditation sitting quite a distance from Amma during the first Devi Bhava in Seattle, I wasn't as attached to being near her. As I was leaving the retreat the next morning, someone asked me if I could take Amma's luggage to the house where she was staying in Seattle. Usually I would have jumped at the chance to get closer to Ammachi. However, this time I asked if someone else wanted to perform this desirable task. I was told that the space in my car was really needed. The directions to Mother's house were not clear and I was a little apprehensive about getting lost in Seattle with Mother's baggage.

I tried to follow closely behind Mother's large, white van as it sped to the ferry. However, devotees kept passing me, desperately attempting to get closer to the van. As I waited in my car to board the ferry, I asked the driver of the car closest to Mother to please change positions since I needed to follow the van. The driver responded, "No way. You're not going to cut in on me." The driver's attitude was that she was going to stay close to Mother at all costs, even if it meant that Amma didn't get her luggage. This behavior reminded me of how a crowd of devotees at the Seattle airport a few days earlier, without awareness, accidentally pushed an elderly man back into the subway car that he was trying to exit at the international gate so that they could be closer to the essence of love and compassion, Amma. I heard that Ammachi once stated that it makes her sick when she sees devotees being rude to others and then *pranam* (bow) in front of her with angelic smiles.

The driver of the car received her negative karma back instantly as she was told to go into a different lane as she tried to follow Amma's van onto the ferry. When she refused to move, the ferry attendant shouted at her that he was going to call the police if she didn't move the car immediately. The devotees who try to cling to Amma's outward form, regardless of whom they hurt, end up spiritually and sometimes physically distant from the Divine.

When I departed the ferry in Seattle, the van I was trying to follow was nowhere to be seen. However, about five minutes later, the van mysteriously appeared right in front of me. I easily followed Amma's motorcade to the right house. I guess when you're delivering a saint's baggage you just can't get lost. When I hold on to Ammachi with love and faith, things always seem to work out; I just cruise while Mother, knowing the Divine directions, drives me to my celestial home.

"Everybody craves attention in the modern age, because attention is food for the ego. However, when the ego arises in the disciple, the guru understands it and immediately corrects him."

Mother is always working on eradicating my ego so that I can eventually merge into God's Infinite Light. During the 1994 tour I didn't have a desire to be in the limelight like I was the previous year when I was in a play. However, as soon as I gave up the desire of being on stage, I was asked to make announcements during the programs. I really didn't want to announce messages and was petrified of speaking extemporaneously in front of hundreds of people daily. However, the only thing that saved me from sounding like a total ignoramus was that, before taking the microphone, I would pray to Mother and ask her to speak through me.

On the first night of the Los Angeles satsang, there were close to a thousand people in attendance, including some famous movie celebrities who were sitting in front of me as I made the announcements. My confidence and ego expanded enormously after playing the role of master of ceremonies in front of Hollywood movie stars that evening. Suddenly I wasn't so frightened of public speaking and decided to create innovative changes that would improve the announcements. I planned on sharing some of my personal experiences with Mother to make the talk more inspiring. The next day when I enthusiastically asked one of the swamis if I should make my usual announcement, he replied that no more announcements were needed in Los Angeles. As soon as my ego got into the act, Mother instantly took the job away.

I was disappointed that I couldn't try out my new egoic announcement techniques. However, later in Los Angeles I finally had an opportunity to demonstrate my new and improved broadcasting abilities. I was calmly eating dinner at the beginning of Devi Bhava during the retreat when one of the devotees rushed in and yelled, "Everyone's been looking for you; Mother wants the announcements made right now." I dropped my plate of Indian delicacies and sprinted the quarter-mile to the darshan hall, while trying to cover up my curry-stained pants.

As I breathlessly entered the crowded darshan hall looking for my crumpled and poorly written notes, I told Swamiji that I was supposed to make an announcement immediately. He passed me the microphone and I slowly began talking in my pseudo-calm and deliberate radio voice as huge drops of sweat poured down my face. When I began my speech, I felt something wasn't right. I didn't think my curry-stained pants were unzipped or the devotees could see my sweating face. The calmer I tried to speak in my hard-breathing state, the more I realized something was definitely wrong. Suddenly, Swamiji grabbed the microphone away from me and simply said, "Someone else just made the same announcement." So much for my famous Hollywood audition.

I had been involved in three theatrical productions during the tour and noticed that Mother would complement others on their performance but she would constantly ignore me. By the time we put on that year's final play at the Boston retreat, I began to feel really confident about my dramatic abilities. In fact, I began counseling the novice performers on various acting techniques.

However, a few days before the performance I kept forgetting my lines. Even on the day of the play I couldn't remember my longest monologue, and simply stood frozen in rehearsal, not having a clue as to what to say. I became terrified that I wouldn't remember my lines on stage, and finally prayed deeply to Mother to help me. Amma took pity on this poor soul and I remembered every word of the dialogue.

I am amazed at the fact that, even though I often become nervous speaking in front of a few people, when I perform in front of Amma and hundreds of devotees, I feel calm and centered. I wish I could always experience Amma's grace flowing through me when I'm acting in the leela of life. God is the doer and whenever my ego thinks "I" can accomplish something by myself, Mother reminds me that any success that I have had in this life is due solely to God's grace.

"How should a real disciple be? He will be the one who serves the guru with the attitude that the guru shouldn't even know about his service."

Since I was busy performing more seva in 1994 and had received many darshans throughout the years, I rarely went up to Amma for a blessing. However, I became jealous when I saw my friends, who sat all day meditating in front of Amma, and who would then tell me about their ecstatic darshan experiences. When I told Mother that I was frustrated seeing most of the other devotees going up for regular blessings, Amma responded, "Mother is aware of and is blessing all her children who are doing seva instead of coming up for darshan." She then added, "There was a king with servants always around, constantly flattering him, but the one who worked hard in the background was the one whom he rewarded." Amma then stated, in her compassionate way, "If you feel like you need a hug, you could come up for darshan."

When I told Amma that I was sad that I didn't spend more time with her because it's difficult for me to travel in India, she responded, "It's all right that you don't spend more time with Mother since you are performing good service." Mother indicated that the benefits that I receive from doing seva for her are equal to being in her physical presence.

The guru is: "the one who wishes to please her devotees by fulfilling all their desires."

Throughout the tour in 1994 I had a secret desire that Mother would say my name. I noticed that she frequently called other devotees by their name and I became jealous. I became excited when I found out that Mother would be flying to Boston from Newark airport since the terminal is only twenty minutes from the house where I grew up. I had a feeling something special might happen there.

When Mother leaves and arrives at an airport, there is usually a huge crowd of devotees to greet her or say good-bye. However, when I arrived at Newark airport, there were only two people waiting for Mother in front of the airline terminal. Although my dad wasn't aware of the tradition of giving flowers to saints, he asked me if I wanted to bring a bouquet of roses from his garden to give to Ammachi. When Mother arrived at the airport, I opened the car door for her and told her that the roses were from my dad as I knelt before her radiant form. She gave me a long hug and smile that transformed my inner being into ecstasy. After the embrace, the two devotees and I guided Ammachi to the gate.

At the terminal there were only about seven disciples sitting around Mother, talking informally as she waited to board the plane. In her omniscient manner of granting me my secret wish by saying my name (and helping me grow spiritually by deflating my ego), Mother looked at me and asked, "Son, what is your name?" I thought of responding, "Mother you know everything, so surely after all these years you must know who I am." However, I nervously mumbled "Dayalu" and she then melodically chanted, "Dayalu, Dayalu, Dayalu." She remarked in passing that the word Dayalu is like Kripalu. Someone from the New York satsang group then started talking about a spiritual community named Kripalu in Massachusetts.

As Mother was about to board her plane, a stewardess came up to Amma and enthusiastically exclaimed in a deep Southern drawl, "I have never seen someone with so much love; I just had to meet you." Naturally Mother gave the airline hostess an angelic embrace. As I stood in the background when Mother was ready to enter the ramp to the plane, she suddenly turned around and shouted, "Dayalu" and came up and hugged me again. Although I drove to Boston, it felt more like I was gliding on the wings of an angel several feet above ground.

During the Boston retreat, I noticed that all of the retreatants (about seven hundred) were lining up for the meditation with Mother. It was to be held in the cafeteria of the college campus since it was raining outside. Since I was just finishing a rehearsal for a play that was to be performed that night, I figured that I would sit in the back of the room because I didn't want to wait in line. Suddenly I saw a huge crowd of people going outside and was told that Mother wanted the meditation at the beach even though it was drizzling. As I went to my car to get my jacket, I saw Mother walking toward the ocean and fortuitously ended up walking in front of her.

When we reached the ocean, Mother started walking carefully on the wet rocks with the crowd following close behind. I sat down on a huge boulder right next to where Mother was standing. It began pouring, so I covered my head with my jacket because I didn't want the Indian shirt I was supposed to wear in the play that night to get soaked. Mother saw what I did and touched my head saying, "Good, cover head." People kept giving Ammachi umbrellas but she would give them back so that they would stay dry and comfortable. She then sat down near me in a perfect full lotus yoga posture.

As soon as Mother closed her eyes, the rain stopped. The waves crashed against the rocks as the fog crept into the shimmering seascape. Every once in a while during the thirty minute meditation, I would hear sacred sounds emanating from Amma. I realized that I couldn't find a much better place to meditate during this incarnation as I dived deeply into God's Light. At the end of the meditation Mother opened her eyes and started

Mother in meditation.

singing to the various forms of God in the sky, ocean and earth. As I beheld my guru's beatific form right in front of me, I thought of the lyrics to a new song that a friend of mine, Shakti, had recently written about Amma:

One glance from you thrills my soul, Sri Kali Amme, Amma
The dance of a trillion worlds in your eyes, Amme, Amma
A trillion worlds, like brilliant pearls in a sea of infinity
A trillion worlds, like brilliant pearls in your eyes, Amme

Dark stars of warning, red skies at morning
A tidal wave storming from the sea of love, Amma

Swept away in an ocean of joy
these mental chains you've come to destroy
Sri Kali, take your sword and set me free

Come break these chains that bind me, Amma
Come take this pain that blinds me, Amma
I love you so much more than words can say

CHAPTER VI

Amma Heals My Childhood

Turn to God...
When troubles come...
Turn to God...Turn to God...
Woes dissolve...
in His bliss, in His Joy.

**"Remember that the master is not simply
going to leave you there all alone. He will help you
by using his infinite spiritual energy.
He will heal your wounds."**

The first time that I went up for darshan with Amma in Seattle in 1995, she looked at me with her eyes wide open and exclaimed, "Dayalu." Compassionately, she remembered to say my name since she knew that last year I had a desire for her to repeat "Dayalu".

During the past winter I had been quite sick with severe bronchial problems. When I asked Mother about the physical difficulties I had been going through, Amma replied, "Not to worry, it's just your *prarabdha* (karma) being burnt up." She added, "Mother made a sankalpa for you so nothing bad will happen." Months of worrying about my poor health seemed to melt away with this simple advice from the Holy Mother.

Again this year I had mixed feelings about performing in a play in front of people. However, I realized that it would be virtually impossible for me with my weak ego, which is always trying to attract attention, to turn down the opportunity for more accolades. When I asked Amma if I should be in a play that year, I felt my soul hoping that she would say no while the egoistic part of me was lobbying for a positive response. I knew that I would feel left out and jealous if other devotees got to perform while I remained a spectator. Mother, knowing what is best for all her children's spiritual growth, gave the perfect answer to help reduce the thespians' egos by simply stating, "There will be no play this year."

On the ferry ride back to Seattle this year, I was again inspired watching Mother go into samadhi, singing to God in the translucent water, the infinite sky and the majestic pine trees. As she concluded the chanting, Ammachi passed out *prasad* (sacred offering) to her beaming children gathered around her in the cold, wet wind. As the Holy Mother dropped a chocolate kiss, I quickly tried to pick it up for her. Amma rushed down to pick up the candy first but in her kindness, stopped and allowed me to retrieve the candy for her.

Inspired by her love, I woke up the next morning singing "*So Hum, So Hum*, Thou (God) and I are one." I didn't stop singing this spiritually uplifting chant throughout the rest of the tour. Thank you, my beloved Amma, for planting this song in my heart.

"Realization is possible only through the eradication of vasanas. The aspirants themselves cannot

**remove their subtle vasanas, they need the guid-
ance, instruction and grace of a Satguru."**

Mother is constantly bringing my vasanas to the surface and
making me look at how destructive my ego is for spiritual growth.
One night when I was doing "parking seva" in San Ramon, I wanted
Amma to notice me as she drove by so that she would be pleased at
the incredibly magnificent job I was doing. I fantasized in the dusty
parking lot, "Why, she may even stop the car, give me a hug and tell
me what a good job I'm doing." I carefully positioned myself to face
toward the direction of Mother's arrival at 7:30 in the evening.

"Ah, here comes Amma's car. Everyone out of the way," I
shouted obnoxiously to the slow drivers as I smiled and pranamed
to my omniscient guru. She literally turned her head away from
me as her car sped by, leaving me covered in a cloud of dust.

On another occasion, I was trying to drive carefully as I
shuttled devotees to the temple on the narrow dirt road. Suddenly, I noticed in my rear view mirror an expensive automobile
being driven in a hurry. The driver passed cars which were patiently waiting in a long line for a parking space. I became infuriated at the nerve of that arrogant, opulent motorist who thought
he was beyond following the rules. As the crowded car sped by
me, I decided to show those rude people a thing or two, by
honking my horn and flashing my bright lights at them. When
one of the passengers exclaimed, "Look, the swamis are in that
car," I felt myself slowly turning a bright red with embarrassment
as my righteous indignation subsided. When I looked at my watch,
I realized that the driver was late for the program that night.

During another evening when I was wearing my parking attendant yellow vest, I was so engrossed in my duties explaining to a driver of a van where he could park, I didn't even notice

Mother arriving at the darshan hall in San Ramon.

Mother's vehicle was being blocked by the van. Mother smiled at me with amusement when I finally noticed her and motioned the car to pass. I finally received Mother's attention when I was performing my seva with concentration.

One day when I was helping out as assistant lap monitor (helping people prepare to receive darshan), I was trying to focus on doing a good job rather than watching Ammachi. While my head was turned away from Amma as I helped some devotees get in line, Mother threw a handful of rose petals on my head, blessing me.

Lap monitors receive a blessing by sitting next to Amma so they generally do not go up for darshan. However, in my egotistic thirst to receive more attention, at the end of the morning program when I saw another lap monitor go up for darshan, I became determined to have my turn and decided to go up next. Just as I arose to put my head on the Holy Mother's lap, she suddenly stood up, looked at me while wiping her hands and exclaimed, "Finished! "

One morning in San Ramon when I was signed up to do parking seva, I was requested to be assistant lap monitor. I rationalized that I had been doing so much seva that at least if I was going to work, I wanted to put in my time at the lotus feet of my beloved guru. I asked a friend of mine to do the parking seva for me but upon returning to the darshan hall, he was dismayed to see me enjoying myself as I sat in front of Mother.

The next day my friend agreed to take a shift selling subscriptions to Amritanandam magazine (the magazine about

Amma). However, when I tried to tell him that his shift was ready to begin, he was sitting in front of Mother and didn't move. I became infuriated with the audacity that someone would agree to do a seva assignment and instead just sit in front of Amma. My anger quickly subsided as I realized, "Oh, oh, that's exactly what I did; instant karma time." Later he told me that he was asked to help out with the line by sitting near Amma.

A few days later, I was asked if I could serve lunch in the kitchen. I had been working hard selling Amritanandam subscriptions all morning and really just wanted to meditate in front of Mother. I agreed to help serve the meals but felt sad that I would miss Amma exit the hall. However, at the end of darshan Mother stopped by at the kitchen and looked at the servers saying, "Seva, seva, seva." She then motioned her hands toward us and then touched her head and repeated, "Karma, karma, karma." She was taking on our karma for doing the seva!

> **"Human effort and God's grace are both necessary. Self-effort is man's half and grace is God's half; yet, without His grace, nothing is possible in spite of efforts put forth. God and medicine, both are needed."**

Traveling with Amma is very difficult for my vata constitution. Vata needs quiet, regularity and going to bed early. Needless to say, the lifestyle on tour is the antithesis of a vata-pacifying life, especially when one considers the monumental amount of energy constantly emanating from the Holy Mother. When I was in Los Angeles, I came up for darshan in a very vulnerable and frightened state. I told Amma that my vata was out of balance which was creating severe physical and emotional problems for me. She took pity on my poor soul and looking at me with deep love, gently rubbed sandalwood paste on my forehead to calm my nervous system. Immediately a sense of peace enveloped me. Tears welled up in my eyes when I realized the depths of how much the Holy Mother loves and comforts me.

During the Los Angeles retreat, I mentioned to Mother that I noticed some of her close disciples have been very sick with chronic illnesses. I asked her, "Since it appears that Mother chooses not to heal these devotees, should they still visit other healers?" Amma responded, " Mother's grace is always with them but if they are sick, they should see a doctor."

Mother is very practical and frequently recommends that the devotees see an ayurvedic or allopathic doctor. A medical course of treatment can be more efficacious for the soul than just saying "my illness is all Mother's will." I realized that I need to have my body functioning at its optimum because when I am sick, I don't have the energy or concentration to do my sadhana efficiently.

I also asked Mother a question concerning emotional healing. I told Mother that even after spending many years with her, I'm still so needy because I was shamed as a child. I told her I was frustrated that I still couldn't let go of my vasanas from childhood. She lovingly responded, "It's good that you are recognizing the situation with the ego, but patience is necessary since it takes a long time to release the ego."

"You cannot be attached to anything in the world and at the same time be at peace, because too much attachment to anything builds up a lot of tension in the mind, and this is bound to create pain."

Whenever I become attached to having a special connection with Ammachi, it invariably becomes a disaster, yet whenever I am detached from receiving her attention, Mother showers me with her radiant love. I had an ecstatic darshan the first time I traveled on a plane with Amma from Chicago to New York two years earlier. After that stratospheric experience in the sky, I became very attached to having personal experiences with Ammachi whenever I flew with her on the same plane.

I was looking forward to being in an intimate group with Amma as we changed planes in Phoenix, flying from Los Angeles to Albuquerque. I relished the thought that there would be no one waiting at the Phoenix airport to greet Ammachi and that we would have the Holy Mother all to ourselves. As we descended into the Phoenix airport, I plotted how I could obtain the closest seat to her as we waited in the terminal for an hour between plane connections.

Like a running back in a championship football game, I huddled with myself on how to quickly get past my opponents, the passengers, and score a touchdown by beating the other devotees to Amma. As I adroitly maneuvered past the opposition, I knew that victory was at hand as I reached the goal line of the nearest seat to Amma. However, to my dismay, as I sat down next to Mother, she playfully interacted with all the other devotees in the waiting area, but totally ignored me as if I were confined to the third string bench. "Hey," I thought to myself, "Don't worry about it... the other devotees probably need the attention more than me." I then created strategies on how I could get close to her on the next flight a few days later from Albuquerque to Dallas.

Ammachi at the airport.

When I finished checking in at the airline counter after spending a sublime five days in Albuquerque, I noticed a crowd of devotees assembling to greet the Holy Mother as she exited the van. I thought to myself, "Ah, let the games begin." During this next sporting event, I decided to out-maneuver the crowd of devotees by making a sneak end-run and stand directly in front

of Amma as she walked through the door into the terminal. I
was proud of the great position I found standing right in front of
Amma as her smiling face lit up the airport lobby. However, what
I thought would result in a brilliant field goal, ended up with me
being penalized again. I became quite frustrated when Mother
turned away from me as soon as she saw my beaming face.

After she totally ignored me, I maturely decided to show
her that two could play this new game and I decided not to pay
any attention to her either. I walked about ten feet in front of
Amma looking for the correct gate, pretending to ignore Mother
as she strolled behind me followed by a multitude of devotees.
However, once I was waiting at the gate I couldn't resist sneaking
a few glances at her as I pouted at the loss of another game.

Although Mother was busy teaching me a lesson, she allowed her love to come to me through the swamis. They are so
filled with Amma's energy that being with them is almost like
being with Mother. On the flight, I was fortunate enough to sit
next to some of the swamis. Unfortunately, there was no dinner
being served on the flight and I was really getting hungry. I looked
around the plane desperately searching for some source of nour-
ishment. Suddenly I noticed one swami handing another a Reese's
peanut butter cup (my favorite treat) that I really wanted. Although
my mouth was salivating like Pavlov's dog, I pretended to read
my spiritually uplifting book. Then the swami opened up the
chocolate and put it in my hand just as if I were receiving prasad
from Mother.

During the tour I had begun helping with the distribution
of the holy water during the Devi Puja. I really wanted to help

with the dispersing of the holy water in Santa Fe but had a premonition that this attachment could create some difficulties. In spite of this ominous feeling, I agreed to perform a new task, picking up the copper bowls filled with water that Mother had blessed and also pouring the holy water into buckets. I would then have to hold the large vessel steady while it was being filled to the brim. Then I'd have to quickly carry the unwieldy con-

Mother blessing Holy Water during Devi Puja.

tainer back to Amma, maneuvering over people seated on the floor. My worst fear was that I would spill the water on Mother or trip while carrying the large copper urn.

It turned out that the most difficult part of the job was trying to balance the large pot with outstretched arms as gallons of water were being poured into the vessel. My hands began shaking slightly as I tried to steady the urn and keep the stream of perspiration flowing from my face from landing in the bowl. I felt utterly helpless in this horrendous predicament and all I could do was repeat my mantra as Amma and the crowd watched the water being poured into the cistern. Fortuitously, with Mother's grace, the worst incident to transpire that evening was that a little water spilled out as I set the copper vessel in front of Amma.

"Once you have surrendered, you do not think about yourself or what others may think about you. You should learn to surrender your ego."

Ammachi had told me a year earlier that I could live in the ashram. In Dallas I told Mother that I felt ashamed because I hadn't moved into the ashram due to a fear of giving up my security. I felt embarrassed because I didn't want to share a room at times during the tour due to insomnia. She replied, "It's all right if you don't want to move into the ashram or share a room during the tour; don't worry about it." However, she added, "It's supposed to be difficult on the tour... It is more expansive for you spiritually if you share a room. Try sharing your room with one person you get along with."

I immediately went up to an old friend and asked him to share my room. We stayed up late that night discussing new approaches to spiritual and emotional healing which subsequently has had a profound impact on my spiritual growth. When I have been able to put my ego and my fears aside and follow Mother's advice, I have evolved both spiritually and emotionally.

"We should live in this world without deviating from the path of dharma even when we are in the midst of life's problems."

The previous year I met a homeless teenager whom I wanted to help. I had loaned this young man money to buy a car but he had stopped making payments on the loan. Many people told me to just let go of the money and it would come back to me in other ways. However, I wanted to act in accordance with dharma for myself, as well as the other person, so I asked Amma how to deal with the situation. Mother asked me, "Did you have a written contract with this person?" When I responded, "Yes," she said, "Keep asking him for the money."

Subsequently when I clearly requested the payments, the money was promptly repaid. In her infinite wisdom, Amma knew what would be the dharmic approach for both the lender and borrower in this case. However, Mother's advice was given solely for me at that particular time.

"The intervals of deep silence, when Mother radiates the bliss of her own inner silence, are of a beauty beyond words."

Even though I only received one darshan from California to Rhode Island, I began to feel that the real darshan with Mother is internal. To be able to always feel Mother's bliss in my heart is my goal. One night during a meditation in Dallas when I least expected it, Mother gave me an experience of the Divine. Although I was trying to relax on the comfortably-cushioned chair in the hotel ballroom, my undisciplined mind was all cranked up, revving at its usual million miles a minute.

All of a sudden, I felt as if a veil disappeared and I was able to transcend the mind. Unexpectedly, different worlds emerged from within me. A door opened and I clearly saw Krishna playing with his disciples; through another passageway I had a vision of Christ... Buddha... Shiva... Rama... Moses... all the saints... the perfect beings were all located in my heart!

Suddenly I became frightened as "I" disappeared in their perfect world. A tiny dead-end road appeared before me which was located on the left side of my head, representing my ego. I understood how I had been identifying with the impermanent little ego instead of the permanent omnipresent Divine. Tears welled up in my eyes as I felt a passionate yearning to identify with God. I felt the ego fighting for survival as it tried to focus on the negativity of this life but simultaneously I observed my connection to the Divine penetrating deeper as it merged into infinity.

As a devotee pushed against me, I watched the mind become angry. I thought to myself, "Why identify with the impermanent ego?" Then I returned to Amma, Krishna, and the other saints living within my heart. I beheld many doorways and mansions deep within, all leading to the Divine.

**"If any one of the sons or daughters of any of
the parents take to spirituality, Mother will
consider it as a great blessing not only for their
family but also for the whole world. By doing so,
he or she is rendering a great service to their
family as well as for the entire human race."**

During the tour, I became attached to the thought of being
blessed with a family member. I had really hoped my son, David,
who I adopted eleven years earlier, would meet me in Santa Fe. I
was disappointed when I discovered that he was unable to travel
there from his home in Boulder, Colorado. Therefore, I became
attached to the notion of receiving a blessing with my dad when
I arrived in New Jersey.

A major issue in my life has been that when I was younger, I
felt my dad was never present for me. When I arrived in New
Jersey, my dad was resistant to receiving darshan from Ammachi,
stating that he'd already seen her. I still hadn't learned that Amma
simultaneously blesses my relatives and friends when I receive
her darshan. I don't have to drag everyone who is important to
me screaming and kicking up to the Holy Mother. I hadn't realized that each soul is on their unique spiritual path and who am
I to interfere with the lessons they have to learn by imposing my
view of spirituality on them?

When I brought my dad to the hotel in New Jersey to get
blessed by Amma, I told him that I wanted us to get blessed together. As we went up together to receive darshan, Amma pulled
my dad's hand so he would receive darshan first. While looking

at me she repeated, "Father, father." When it was my turn to receive the blessing, father kept moving farther and farther away. As I was laying on Ammachi's lap, I was literally pulling my dad's arm forward so we could get blessed together as he kept pulling away. Mother witnessed this father/son tug-of-war which was a metaphor for my relationship with him, but she chose not to intervene. Ah, another attachment gone astray with the Holy Mother.

However, Amma compassionately stated, " Mother is very pleased when she sees her children taking care of their older parents." As I got up from the Holy Mother's lap, my dad dashed to the exit. I finally understood that although I have a bond during this incarnation with my birth family, my real home is with the Divine, which is my home for eternity.

"We are caught in the illusion that we will get happiness from the world. Then we madly run here and there, craving to acquire it. Having unfulfilled desires, frustration and anger results. However, when we awaken to God-consciousness, we will realize the world to be a dream."

I have spent a good part of my adult life trying to heal early childhood wounds. Amma, the ultimate Divine surgeon, created a scenario in New Jersey for the removal of some of my deepest vasanas. I felt guided to contact an old friend whom I hadn't seen in twenty-five years when I visited the New York area on tour in 1995. For a long time I wanted my old friend, Alan (and others like him), to approve and accept me exactly as I am.

As I waited nervously in front of the Frank Lloyd Wright-designed estate, I spotted my old college roommate driving up in an expensive red sports car. I thought to myself that Alan had surely succeeded in achieving the "American dream" and began to wonder what I had really attained in my life. Even though I tried to dedicate myself to finding God, I still felt like a failure for not being married or owning my own home. I became embarrassed and began creating a strategy on how I would answer my friend's questions to make myself look successful so that he would approve of me.

With excuses for my fruitless life in hand, I entered Alan's palatial estate. However, when I finally began talking honestly with my old acquaintance, I was struck by the emptiness that I observed in his life. Even though he had a lovely wife and a magnificent mansion, his pain and loneliness became self-evident. Alan shared with me how upset he was that his wife had thought of leaving him and the difficulties he had been experiencing with his children. His endless search of trying to find happiness by buying one expensive "toy" after another only seemed to create a deeper state of ennui. When I left his enormous, yet sterile home that evening, I realized that his acceptance of me really didn't matter. Instead, I just wanted to be able to give him some love and support.

After that insightful experience, I returned to visit my old junior and senior high schools which had been a major source of humiliation for me. I was surprised to see new signs posted all over Roosevelt Junior High School stating, "Encounters should be made with mutual respect, courtesy and cooperation." As I turned the corner to exit the building, I noticed a huge sign addressed to the teachers from the students that stated, "I am growing and changing and have feelings and want to be respected and most of all I want to be heard by you." Suddenly I heard some phrases from the John Lennon song, "Imagine", being played on the radio in the background. I gazed down the dimly-lit corridor listening to the words: "Imagine all the people living life in peace... imagine all the people sharing all the world... I hope some day you'll join us and the world will live as one." I saw a sunbeam descending from a skylight flowing through the hallway and I knew the past had shifted and the Light is penetrating everywhere on the planet.

As I basked in the sunlit hallway, I realized that my impermanent flesh which grows new cells every seven years can't be defined solely by my childhood experiences. The parameters of who I think I am are expanding and changing. I felt myself coalescing into a Divine timeless energy of the past, present and future. When I finally departed the institution of "higher learning", I joyfully sang to myself, "So Hum, So Hum, God and I are one, Thou and I are one."

My healing pilgrimage continued as I visited my mother's grave for the first time since I attended the funeral two years earlier. As I got out of my gray rental car, a soft rain began falling from the dark, cloudy sky. When I finally found my mom's grave, I cleared away some dry grass and weeds from the tombstone and sat down to meditate in the warm, gentle rain. I felt that my mom's soul was finally at peace and contemplated how everyone's body will, sooner than we think, end up either buried underground or cremated. I thought to myself, "How foolish I've been to have spent so much time being worried about my outward physical appearance which will dissolve into the earth in a few years."

I remembered a verse from a song that Amma sang: "Even your beloved who said she would always love you, will turn away from your dead body." Everyone who says they will love us forever will leave except God. After some time I slowly got up, pranamed to the grave, and softly walked away contemplating the impermanence of this body. I realized that the only thing really important in life is the Divine love that people share with each other.

The previous year at Newark Airport, I had a most ecstatic satsang with Mother since hardly anyone showed up to greet her. Throughout the tour, I was hoping to repeat that intimate experience with Amma. However, I still hadn't learned that attachment only creates failure. Right before I left for the airport to see Amma, my dad finally revealed a secret about how I was physically abused by a family member as an infant. Although I was shocked to hear the story, I was still looking forward to receiving an inspiring darshan with Amma within an hour. However, when I arrived at the airport, I was told that Mother had driven to Boston after Devi Bhava the night before. My rider found out that Amma wasn't coming to the airport and subsequently never showed up. I then had to drive to Boston alone, brokenhearted that I missed Mother and in shock about the disturbing news that I just learned about my early childhood.

As I drove to Boston, I noticed an exit sign in Connecticut for a town named New Britain. I remembered that I lived briefly in this small city as an infant and as a very young child. Although it was my first visit to this little town in more than forty years, I was able to find the three story white clapboard corner house that I used to live in. As I strolled around the three-family home, peering into the first-floor windows, a flood of memories surfaced which helped me to integrate the recent news that I had just heard about my painful past.

As I peeked into the large, bright kitchen at the rear of the house, I remembered watching my mom make star-shaped cookies with old-fashioned metal cookie-cutters as I joyfully waited for the delicacies to be baked in the sweet-scented, sunny kitchen... the beveled, frosted bathroom window reminded me of the pain and fear I felt when I accidentally fell on the bathroom tiled floor from the wash basin and being rushed to the hospital where I received five stitches above my right eye... memories of the mixture of terror and joy relating to a disturbed parent emerged... a gentle, yet distant recollection of my mother asking me "Why are you such a good boy?" as I sat at the oak dining room table... my innocent response, "Because you love me, mommy" ...the memory of the delight and warmth I felt watching sunbeams flow through the large bedroom window laced with green curtains as I lay on my teddy-bear-laden bed with a mother who's grave I visited yesterday.

As I entered my rental car full of nostalgic feelings, I noticed a baby-blue tricycle propped up against the white two-car garage and remembered how dejected and hurt I felt when my little bicycle had been stolen from that exact spot almost a half-century earlier. I took a deep breath and thought about how some things may have been taken away from me while I was growing up, but no one could ever remove my desire for the Divine Truth.

I remained quiet and inward during the Boston programs but by the time I arrived at the pastoral college campus in Rhode Island for the final retreat of 1995, I was still filled to the brim with heart-wrenching emotions. I decided to offer all these memories, these vasanas, at the feet of the Holy Mother. As I approached Amma in the question line at the huge college gymnasium, she gave me a mesmerizing and compassionate look. It seemed as if she were looking directly into the deepest recesses of my soul as she told me, "Son, everything's all right, I'm always with you."

"Children will have a natural attraction to their mother and a mother will be naturally loving and compassionate towards her children and will look after their needs. This is the case with the Divine Mother also."

Amma intuitively knew I didn't sleep well the first night of the retreat and immediately asked me when I went up for darshan, " Tired?" She then began stroking my chin and forehead. I knelt before Amma, offering all of my anguish and suffering of this life, as well as all my other past lives, at the feet of the Holy Mother. Tears suddenly began streaming down my cheeks like a broken faucet and I couldn't find a wrench to repair the faulty pipe in my consciousness as a flood of salt water spewed forth.

Amma compassionately told me, "Keep saying your mantra if you are nervous or have trouble sleeping. It was your karma to choose a difficult family situation to be born into and the trauma you experienced as an infant left some minor nervous problems." She added, "Do not worry because Mother is doing a sankalpa to help you overcome what happened. If you pray for your biological mother's soul and forgive her, she will not have to suffer for anything she did when she was in the body. Now you have Amma as your Mother so forget about the past."

My beloved Guru then began rubbing sandalwood paste on my forehead to cool down my overheated nervous system. As I sat down to meditate after darshan, I kept thinking to myself, "Oh, how blessed I am to have Mata Amritanadamayi as my Mother for eternity. Amma, how can I ever thank you for giving me, your poor child, so much comfort? Oh my beloved Amma, stay in my heart forever. I love you so much."

"Patience is needed to make spiritual progress. Do your spiritual practices with utmost sincerity and wait patiently. If you are sincere, the results will come."

In 1993 I asked Amma if I could move into the ashram in San Ramon and she responded in the affirmative. I immediately told my friends that Mother said I could move into the ashram so I could impress them as to how spiritual I had become. However, with my need for security and tranquillity, I knew there was no way I would ever give up my home, possessions, dog, and independence, to live in an ashram.

Toward the end of the 1993 tour Swami Paramatmananda, the resident swami in San Ramon, said, "Dayalu, I heard you're moving into the ashram." Knowing it wasn't really the truth, I replied, "Who spread that ridiculous rumor?" When he responded, "Amma told me," I thought to myself, "Dayalu, you really better watch your step now or you're going to end up in big doggy-doo." I very quickly changed the subject, wondering whether I had created some bad karma for myself.

I tend to become impatient unless my desires are fulfilled immediately and have a difficult time accepting delays. Although I didn't want to live in the ashram, for several years I had been trying to find a house to rent with other devotees in San Ramon but had not been successful. Perhaps the lack of success was due partly to the fact that I was reticent to give up my quiet retreat home in the mountains to relocate to what I considered to be the polluted, congested and noisy Bay Area.

I thought that once I rented a house, I would be able to find a devotee with whom to share the house. In 1994 when I asked Amma about the difficulties I was experiencing finding a house, she responded, "It may still happen; find the devotee first and then find the house." That year she gave me hope that I still would be able to move closer to the ashram, as well as specific instructions on how the move could be accomplished. However, by not following Amma's advice of finding the devotee first rather than looking for a house on my own, I created frustrations and delays in the move.

After two years of looking for the perfect house near the ashram whereby I could keep my dog and possessions, I became quite frustrated. However, Amma knew how to guide my soul's evolution for its ultimate highest good while taking into consideration my ego's powerful cravings. From Mother's perspective, spending a few years preparing for an important spiritual change is fine, but with my lack of patience, I just couldn't accept the Divine timing. I wanted Mother to find the perfect living situation for me right now.

I had been advised that, astrologically, the Fall of 1995 was an auspicious time to make a move. During the previous year I tried to spend one week at the ashram every month and was slowly getting used to being in the Bay Area again. Finally, in September of that year I decided to make an all-out effort to find a house, staying at the ashram for one month. After unsuccessfully trying to look for a reasonably-priced house that would accept a dog, I became quite discouraged and decided to give up the search. I resigned myself to continue living in the Nevada City area.

However, the day before I went to see Amma in New York where she addressed the 50th anniversary of the United Nations, a devotee asked me if I was still interested in sharing a house. Although I had given up hope in ever finding a house near the ashram, after his inquiry I happened to look in the newspaper that evening and found an exquisite home for rent. The owner immediately rented us the palatial home in San Ramon with my dog, Karma, et al.! What came to pass was just as Mother predicted when she told me one and a half years earlier that I should find the roommate first, then look for a house, and that the move could still happen.

I was now about to make the long-awaited move to the Bay Area after living for eleven years in the Sierra mountains (and the last eight years in my own secluded mountain-top home). First, however, I was off to see Mother in New York City.

It was like a dream being with Mother in New York in October since previously I had only seen Amma in the summertime. I was blessed to be with a small group of people who were invited to meet with Mother in a living room of a devotee's apartment when she arrived in New York. I've had many splendid dreams of spending time with Amma in an informal setting where she is continuously showering her Divine love on me. Unfortunately, just when I am ready to receive a hug from her, the alarm clock goes off thrusting me back to the earth plane. (Perhaps my nocturnal trysts with God were more real than turning off the annoying buzzer next to my bed).

It was so inspiring to have a living saint lead us in the blessing over the food and chat with us informally. As I descended in the Manhattan apartment building elevator after the short satsang, I had to pinch myself to make sure the rendezvous with Amma had really happened.

I returned to California renewed with Amma's Divine energy to make my move to San Ramon. I felt a mixture of sadness yet appreciation towards the members of the Yogananda spiritual community which I was about to leave after more than a decade. I decided to write a farewell letter to the community which stated:

> "I am moving to the Bay Area to be at Ammachi's ashram. I want to thank you all for your spiritual

*support these past eleven years that has helped me
to progress toward the goal of Self-Realization.
Therefore, with joined palms, I pranam to all of
you shining souls. I love you and will miss you very
much.*

"*Just as the river may break off into thousands of
tributaries, merge for awhile again then form a
multitude of new waterways; still the little drop-
lets are always flowing toward the mighty ocean.
So my dear brothers and sisters in God, may we all
meet again soon as we merge into that sea of Divine love of our glorious Mother-Father-God where
bubbles of names and differences dissolve into the
one incandescent Light. Until then, may each and
everyone of you be healthy and happy throughout
your spiritual journey.*"

Although the move went exceedingly well and I enjoyed
the luxury of my modern, spacious home equipped with a hot
tub, swimming pool and instant hot water from the kitchen
sink, I felt awkward not living a more Spartan life in the ashram.
After a few months of residing in my luxurious home, I felt a
powerful, magnetic force pulling me to move into the ashram.

I really didn't want to give up my lovable hound-dog,
Karma, but I found myself visiting several potential doggy
homes. My exceedingly well- behaved, house-broken pet man-
aged to leave little souvenirs on expensive carpets everywhere
we visited. I realized that some "karmas" are harder to give up
than others. However, the day I became clear that I really had

to let go of my Karma, I found him a good home with "parental" visitation rights.

I felt sad but in my heart I knew that ultimately the letting go would set us both free. A few months later when Amma was

My second dog Karma.

in San Ramon in June, 1996, I brought my big, black hound to the ashram and stood very far back as Mother was leaving the morning program. I could tell that Amma was tired but she still came up to us and gave prasad to both "Karma" and myself.

Within the first two weeks of February, I had let go of my dog, put my possessions in storage and moved into the ashram. Amma was right when she told Swami Paramatmananda that I was going to move into the ashram years earlier. She just needed some time to let some air out of my inflated attachment balloon.

CHAPTER VII

In The Ashram

I'm going so far away
leaving behind all my earthly dreams...
flying home through the stars
into Thy loving arms...
melting into Thy love
now and forever more.

"A Perfect Master always protects the aspirant."

Although life in the ashram was intense preparing for Mother's visit, I felt like I was living in the Divine Mother's vibration, wrapped in her loving arms. I was able to experience Ammachi's vibration during the daily programs and by living with other devotees who were focused on Divine Mother. Amma has said that the ashram is the body of the guru.

For two months prior to the 1996 tour, I was going through a very difficult astrological period with challenging physical and emotional issues. When I saw Amma during the first darshan in Seattle, I poured out my heart to her, sobbing uncontrollably. She stroked my face gently and gave me the most compassionate look. Although I was living in the ashram, it felt so good to finally be comforted, in person, on the lap of the Holy Mother.

I hurt my back two months prior to the tour and had seen a multitude of healers who all told me to do various stretches. Mother, the ultimate Divine physician, gave me a specific prescription: "Do not do any stretching or yoga postures; just use herbs and oils and do not see any more healers. Mother will say a special prayer for the injury." Evidently I had torn a tendon or ligament, so the stretching only aggravated the pain. The x-rays that were taken by an orthopedist couldn't detect what Mother's x-ray vision could see.

After Mother answered my question I was amazed watching how she simultaneously answered other questions, blessed people, smiled at the musicians and gave energy to devotees. Later that night I noticed Mother repeatedly signaling for someone to come up. I kept looking around but didn't see anyone. Finally, I noticed that Amma's x-ray vision spotted a shy girl standing next to a pillar at the very rear of the hall. I went up to her and asked if she wanted darshan and she bashfully responded yes.

In Seattle, I asked Amma if I should utilize an affirmation that I had used previously that seemed to help me contradict old negative patterns. To release the pessimistic programming that I felt worthless, I used to repeat "I love and approve of myself." I asked Mother about this technique.

At first I didn't understand why Amma laughed when she heard this question. Later I realized how silly it must have sounded to Mother, who is always trying to break down my ego, to ask if I should constantly repeat "I love myself, I love myself" However, after chuckling, she replied, " It is fine to repeat this affirmation and you could also add that Mother loves and approves of you."

"For your deep, age old wounds, you need an all-knowing, Divine doctor. A real master is absolutely necessary, someone who can see into all your past lives, who knows how to treat and cure your inner wounds."

When I arrived in Los Angeles, for some reason unbeknown to me, I couldn't stop thinking of emotional pain from my past. Finally I asked Mother a few questions: "Why am I feeling sadness and a lack of inspiration? Why can't I seem to meditate in Mother's presence?" Amma responded, "Mother is bringing up your deep-rooted sadness and pain. You don't feel so inspired this year because you're not spending as much time with Mother. Sit closer to Amma and the inspiration will return."

When I sat near Amma, singing passionately to God that evening, I felt some of the Divine joy return. Later, I asked Amma about what life was going to be like in the astral plane when I leave my body. I told her that I hope it's not as painful as life on the Earth plane. She replied, "As long as you keep offering everything to Divine Mother, you will have nothing to worry about in the astral plane."

Her response only confirmed my belief that the more I dive deeply into a dharmic, spiritual life while in the body, my soul will be at peace in the astral plane. Amma's advice inspired me to treat all sentient beings in a kind and empathetic manner. I then made a resolve to take responsibility for my behavior and to be aware of how my words and actions affect other people.

When Mother told me that she was bringing up all my deep-rooted sadness, I realized that it would allow me to experience and release deep primal pain. Swami Amritaswarupananda told me that when we are going through a difficult emotional period while in Mother's presence, the catharsis becomes a purification.

At the Los Angeles retreat Mother asked me many questions about an ashram resident who did not go on tour and was also going through a difficult emotional period. When I called the ashramite and told him about Amma's concern, he said that hearing that Amma had inquired about him was truly a life saver. He was very depressed since Mother left San Ramon and desperately needed to know that she was with him. Of course, Ammachi knew how to lift his spirits even from four hundred miles away.

A vedic astrologer told me in San Ramon that during the tour I would want to be alone. I thought that it wouldn't be possible because I would have to be with so many people, but Divine Mother evidently had other plans for me. When I left Los Angeles, I came down with a bad flu and by the time I arrived in Santa Fe I had a fever, and was sneezing and coughing. However, the illness turned out to be a blessing in disguise because I had an opportunity to be alone and to process all of the emotional trauma that I was experiencing. I felt that Mother guided me to an excellent acupuncturist and herbalist resulting in a speedy recovery whereby I was well enough to be able to perform in a play during the Santa Fe retreat.

Mother created many magical moments for me in Santa Fe that helped me understand that her spiritual energy is with me wherever I go. The person I was staying with in Santa Fe wanted a copy of a fairly obscure book I was reading called "Living and Leaving the Good Life." I walked to a nearby used bookstore and asked the salesperson if they knew where I could find the book. The clerk surprisingly replied that a few hours ago someone just had brought in a copy of the exact book that I wanted, in excellent condition! The last thing that I wrote down in my journal that morning about healing myself was that I had to become my own father. As I opened a book randomly in the bookstore, I was amazed to find a chapter entitled "How to become your own father!"

The next day I became discouraged when I couldn't find a ride to the Devi Bhava and decided that I just wouldn't go. As soon as I made that decision, someone offered me a ride to the evening program. I was also frustrated that I couldn't arrange transportation to the airport the next day. While I was eating dinner, someone sitting next to me told me that her plane was leaving the same time as mine and offered me a ride. After these synchronistic experiences I was beginning to have a little more faith in the Divine.

However, later that evening I felt some flu symptoms returning. By 2:00 a.m. I wanted to go home but could not find a ride. I decided to stand in front of the darshan tent and ask people if they were going into town. After waiting for fifteen minutes, a man agreed to take me to the house where I was staying. It was extremely dark in the rural area where the program was held and there was a new moon that night. After wandering around the parking areas for more than a half an hour, the man who volunteered to drive me home began uttering strange comments such as "It's fine if we never find the car." When I suggested that we look for a flashlight, he responded in a sardonic manner, "I don't need your nervousness." At that point I left him and after another twenty minutes finally made my way back to the darshan hall.

It was now after 3:00 a.m. and I felt really sick, scared and angry. I decided to go up for darshan but while I was in line I kept planning how to arrange a ride home as soon as Amma blessed me. My mind was spinning out of control as I became frightened that I had no way to return to the house. When I went up for the blessing, Amma gave me the longest and sweetest darshan of the tour and then in a very loud voice unequivocally stated, "Sit down, now" while pointing right next to her. I still wanted to look for a ride but decided to

follow the guru's instructions, so I sat down. I quickly entered a deep and tranquil meditative state that lasted for about thirty minutes. The moment I opened my eyes someone tapped me on the shoulder and asked if I'd like a ride home! Afterwards, I remembered that exactly a year earlier I also had no ride home after Devi Bhava in Santa Fe and after an ecstatic meditation next to Amma, when I opened my eyes, I was asked if I needed a ride.

When I arrived in Chicago, I didn't realize that Amma had more emotional release in store for me. I wasn't able to have my questions answered during the first morning program. However, the next day I left my niece Rebecca's house bright and early and planned on having a long day with Mother since it was also a Devi Bhava night. As I calmly drove on the freeway to the program site, all of the sudden, the car swerved back and forth across the highway and I was barely able to maintain control of the vehicle. It was miraculous that the car did not smash into any other cars. I immediately got off at the next exit and realized to my dismay that I had two rear flat tires and no spare. To make matters worse, I was stranded in one of the worst ghettos in Chicago.

In this rather dangerous and difficult leela, I began repeating my mantra and praying to Amma. Instead of abandoning the car and walking through a dangerous gang-infested neighborhood, I decided to try to maneuver the car to the nearest gas station. Passing by a formidable-looking housing project laden with broken glass and angry-looking young men drinking from their morning bottle of cheap red wine, I still felt that I was safe in Mother's arms. Upon entering the service station, I was greeted by hostile people accosting me for money. Although I was anxious, I felt Mother's presence strongly and knew everything would turn out all right.

After waiting for hours in the gas station, I was finally able to have the car towed back to my niece Rebecca's house. So much for spending the day with Ammachi. The next day I was to fly to New Jersey and stay in the family house in West Orange that was filled with many disturbing childhood memories, the worst being in 7th grade. Since I wasn't able to return to the program, Rebecca and I went to see a movie entitled "Welcome to the Doll House" which turned out to be about a Jewish 7th grader from West Orange, New Jersey who was abused in school and at home. As I watched my life unfold in front of me on the screen, I realized that Ammachi wasn't kidding around when she told me that she was bringing up all my old pain.

When I arrived in New Jersey, I found out that my dad had been admitted to the hospital the previous day. He had a blood clot in his brain which the doctors dissolved with a blood thinner but he was still in bad shape. Since he had deteriorated so much physically, I asked Amma when he was going to die. Amma said that he has a lot of physical problems and she gave a specific time period when he would probably leave his body. However, she added that if he should survive that period, he could live another three years.

I also asked her why it has been so difficult for me recently and she responded, "You have been going through a difficult karmic period the last three months and it will continue for about

another three and a half months, then the physical and emotional problems will heal. The difficulties you've been encoun-
tering show how transitory the body and mind are; the Divine is
our true nature." When I left the question line, I thought to
myself that I need to be less attached to the multitude of physical
and emotional problems I'm facing but understand that God is
my only reality.

The morning after the Devi Bhava in New York, I found my
dad lying at the bottom of the stairs mumbling incoherently. He
couldn't walk without falling down and I knew that he could not be
left alone anymore. Although I was distraught that my dad's physical
body was falling apart, I noticed how God's timing had allowed me
to attend the New York programs since I had previously planned on
helping my dad by not going to see Amma in Boston. During the
next two whirlwind days, I had to find a nursing facility, full time
immediate care, arrange power of attorney, a living will and put the
house that the family had for thirty-eight years up for sale. Only
through God's grace could I have completed all these emotionally-
charged tasks in a calm and efficient manner.

Once I completed all of the laborious familial tasks, I re-
gretfully had to leave for the Rhode Island retreat and then fly
back to California. As I departed the home I grew up in for the
last time, I experienced a sense of nostalgia. However, I also felt
relief that I could now finally leave the past behind. The movers
would come soon to disassemble the museum-like shelves my mom
had created to proudly display the Etruscan art objects purchased
in Italy; the golden Sabbath candlesticks my grandmother car-
ried from Poland would be neatly stored in moving boxes; the

Salvation Army employees would pick up the plastic-covered white living room couch that the children were not allowed to sit on, as well as my little wastepaper basket with the pictures of boys playing football and baseball. A lifetime of possessions quickly dispersed to the four winds as my dad, like his mother before him, would end up spending his remaining days in one little room with faded pictures of family members decorating the wall; a last attempt to hold on to human love before departing the Earth plane forever.

As I entered the airport bus, I contemplated how smoothly the hectic last few days had flowed. Amma forged my way through the ocean and ferried me safely past the lighthouse into the harbor of Divine grace. Without living a spiritual life, my final departure from West Orange would have been excruciatingly painful. It felt as if Amma helped my spirit to dive deep and allowed me to face a monumental task in a calm, focused manner.

> **"We realize our limitations when we are in the presence of a Mahatma, whose infinite dimensions and unlimited love and compassion help us to feel humble."**

In response to a question I asked Mother about starting a new business during the retreat, she stated, "Mother blesses your career but you should do more spiritual practices to increase your mental strength." She then told me to frequently repeat the affirmation "I am the *Atman* (one with the Divine), nothing can harm me."

Mother never misses an opportunity to deflate my ego so that I will eventually reach the goal of merging into the Divine. As long as I think that I'm special, I am separating myself from God. Before I went up to get blessed during Devi Bhava, I mentioned to a friend while standing at the back of the crowded gymnasium that Mother had been smearing sandalwood paste all over my forehead every time I'd gone up for darshan since last year. I told my friend, "I'm going to go up for darshan now, so watch how Mother smears me with sandalwood." Naturally when I went up for a blessing, she didn't put any sandalwood on my forehead, letting me know that she is aware of every one of my egotistic thoughts.

"A Mahatma is filled with compassion when he sees a leper. He will not feel disgust or aversion. Through concentration and Divine power he can absorb the disease into himself."

Throughout the tour I had asked Mother on three different occasions to help me heal my back, which had been creating a great deal of physical and emotional pain for more than three months. Although she had given me some suggestions, my back had only improved slightly. In a final desperate attempt, I groveled, pleaded and begged at the feet of the Holy Mother for her to help heal me during my last darshan in Rhode Island. She responded, "It will get better." I felt a sense of relief knowing that some day I would be pain free again.

I decided to take a brief nap after receiving Mother's final darshan during Devi Bhava. I woke up at 5 a.m. so I could spend the last few hours with my beloved Guru before she departed for Europe. I was so charged with her Divine vibrations, in spite of a lack of sleep, that I foolishly helped load the truck at the end of the program at seven in the morning. Once the truck was packed, I realized the utter stupidity of my carrying heavy items, even though my back felt better. Although I thought that I could have reinjured my back, I hoped that Mother's energy could have nullified the laws of science in this case. Upon arising the next morning, I was pleasantly surprised to find that my back felt better than it had since before the injury. I inwardly said to Amma, "Oh Mother... joy, joy, joy... you have given me so much joy!" It seems that Ammachi decides when to heal her children according to God's Divine law.

"The guru's words must be listened to with great attention and devotion."

In November, 1996, Amma made a surprise six day visit to the San Ramon ashram, her only stop in the United States. When she arrived at the ashram to greet the residents, Amma looked at me and mentioned, "Sometimes I call him Dayalu and sometimes I call him Kripalu." Needless to say, I was elated that Mother showered some of her Divine attention on me. I was rather ecstatic to hear that Mother refers to me as Dayalu, let alone by another name. That one statement made my day and actually made my week with Mother!

Later that afternoon, I was contemplating on why she said sometimes she calls me Kripalu. Suddenly I remembered that three and a half years earlier when I saw Amma at the Newark airport, she said to me that the name Dayalu is like Kripalu. When I try to rationally figure out how Mother could remember every detail of the hundreds of thousands of people she blesses, I become awe-struck at how my infinitesimal mind can not even begin to conceive of the magnitude of the Divine.

While Amma's visit was physically exhausting for me, as I was working around the clock like the other devotees, I felt in-

Amma arriving at the San Ramon ashram.

credibly spiritually uplifted. Unfortunately, right after Amma's departure I became very sick with a bad flu that lasted for more than three weeks. I had planned to visit Ammachi's ashram in India at the end of December, and was concerned whether I should make such an arduous journey in such a weakened state. Therefore, I consulted two vedic astrologers less than a week before my departure date. Both astrologers said that my planetary configuration could not be in a worse position for international travel. They warned me that I would become very sick, have severe emotional problems and be absolutely miserable if I went to India the following week. The astrological reading really frightened me about traveling during such an inauspicious time.

Even though the astrologers told me to postpone the trip, I really had my heart set on finally seeing Amma in India. Therefore, I decided to ask Mother what to do and was able to get a response from her in India. I made a resolve that if Mother said to come to India, I was going to make the trip on faith no matter what the astrologers told me. However, if Amma did not encourage me to go, I would not make the pilgrimage. On the climactic day before the scheduled journey, I finally received the response: "If it's a bad time for you and there's fear now, don't feel that you have to come." Although feeling sad and ashamed about not going to India, the decision not to make the trip felt completely right.

Although I didn't see Mother in India, I felt her grace flow through me as I embarked on my journey of writing these reminiscences of her. When I focused on the Divine through the medium of writing, I became filled with Divine love each day.

When I would sit at my computer trying to move my ego out of the way, I would feel God's grace flowing through me.

My thirst for God increases by the day as I try to abstain from drinking out of the mundane mug of maya and instead sip from the celestial spirit. I need to constantly behold Amma's radiant form and focus on the Divine regardless of where I am or what state I'm in. I know in my heart of hearts that only this truth can ever bring me lasting inner peace and joy.

"No matter what condition, country or form,
always sing God's name.

No matter what work, profession or village, always
sing God's name.

No matter what company, color, or emotion,
always sing God's name.

No matter what path of yoga, sense pleasure or
disease, always sing God's name."

—"Jisa Hale Me"
(Traditional Indian spiritual song)

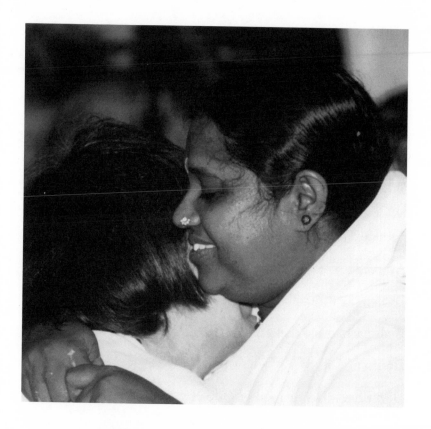

"Don't worry children, Mother is always with you."

GLOSSARY

Adharma: Unrighteous behavior

Avatar: Incarnation of God

Ashram: The home of a group of people who lead a spiritual life; generally the home of a spiritual teacher

Atman: The Eternal Self; God

Ayurveda: The ancient healing system of India

Bhajan: Devotional singing

Brahmacharya: a celibate spiritual aspirant

Darshan: Audience of a holy person

Devi Bhava: Divine mood or identity with the Goddess; the Divine Mother

Devotee: One who has faith in God or a specific saint

Dharma: righteous behavior in accordance with Divine Harmony

Divine Mother: A manifestation of God in the feminine form

Dosha: physical constitution

Hari Bol: Sing to God

Harmonium: An organ-like keyboard instrument with small metal reeds

Jai: victory

Ji: used as a form of respect at the end of a name

Kali: Goddess of destruction and transformation

Krishna: Incarnation of Lord Vishnu

Krishna Bhava: Divine mood or identity with Krishna

Kurukshetra: Battle site from the Bhagavad Gita

Leela: Divine play

Mahasamahdi Mandir: site where a saint consciously left his body and merged into God

Mahatma: Great soul

Mantra: a sacred syllable(s) or phrase

Mata: Mother

Mata Amritanandamayi: Ammachi's formal name; mother of immortal bliss

Maya: Power of universal illusion that makes the world seem real

Moksha: See Realization

Pitta: Fire constitution in Ayurveda

Prarabdha: Karma; Action seen as bringing upon oneself inevitable results either in this life or previous births

Pranam: To bow with folded hands

Prasad: Sacred offering, usually food

Puja: Ritual worship, ceremony

Rajasic: Hyperactive, restless

Realization: The state of complete identity with God

Sadhak: A spiritual seeker

Sadhana: Spiritual practices

Samadhi: State of absorption in God

Sankalpa: Resolve

Sannyasin: A renunciate monk

Satguru: Realized spiritual master

Satsang: Spiritual gathering; spiritual discourse by a saint or scholar

Self: God; one's spiritual essence not identified with body or mind

Seva: Selfless service

So Hum: Sanskrit for God and I are one

Sri Chakra: The Universal Mother

Tamasic: Low energy; dull

Tapas: Spiritual austerities

Vasanas: Latent tendencies of the mind resulting from prior actions

Vata: Air constitution in Ayurveda

OTHER BOOKS ABOUT AMMACHI

AMMACHI: A BIOGRAPHY OF MATA AMRITANANDAMAYI

AWAKEN CHILDREN, VOLUMES 1-8
(Ammachi's inspiring conversations with spiritual seekers)

COME QUICKLY DARLING CHILDREN
(Stories by Western devotees of Ammachi)

FOR MY CHILDREN
(Mother's selected teachings)

GETTING TO JOY
(A Western householder's spiritual journey with Amma)

IMMORTAL LIGHT
(Advice to householders)

ON THE ROAD TO FREEDOM
(A Westerner's twenty-five year spiritual journey)

PUJA
(Instructions on how to perform ritual worship)

Available at your local bookstore or may be ordered from:

AMMACHI PUBLICATIONS
P.O. BOX 613
SAN RAMON, CA 94583
TEL: 510-537-9467 or 888-524-2662

Audio and video tapes are also available from Ammachi Publications

RESOURCES

UNITED STATES ASHRAM:

There are Ammachi satsang groups that meet regularly in 42 cities in 20 states throughout the United States and in 5 cities in Canada. Please call the M.A. Center in San Ramon, California at 510-537-9417 for information regarding local Ammachi groups in North America.

AUSTRALIA:

For information on Ammachi satsang groups, please contact James Conquest; 278 Orrong Rd. Caulfield NTH Vic. 3161 Melbourne 03- 95259957.

EUROPE:

For information on Ammachi satsang groups throughout Europe, please contact Maison Amrita, BP 88. F68160, Ste. Marie Aux Mines, France (international code +) 338-958-5956.